SEVENTH
Leveraged ESOPs
and Employee Buyouts

Regina Carls
Philip J. Carstens
Vaughn Gordy
Dan Kaczmarek
William Merten
Scott Rodrick
Corey Rosen
David Solomon

The National Center for Employee Ownership
Visit us at **www.nceo.org** for more information about ESOPs

This publication is designed to provide accurate and authoritative information in regard to the subject matter covered. It is sold with the understanding that the publisher is not engaged in rendering legal, accounting, or other professional service. If legal advice or other expert assistance is required, the services of a competent professional person should be sought.

Legal, accounting, and other rules affecting business often change. Before making decisions based on the information you find here or in any publication from any publisher, you should ascertain what changes might have occurred and what changes might be forthcoming. The NCEO's website (including the members-only resources) and newsletter for members provide regular updates on these changes. If you have any questions or concerns about a particular issue, check with your professional advisor or, if you are an NCEO member, call or email us.

Leveraged ESOPs and Employee Buyouts, Seventh Edition
Book design by Scott Rodrick

Copyright © 2020 by The National Center for Employee Ownership. All rights reserved. No part of this book may be reproduced or transmitted in any form or by any means, electronic or mechanical, including photocopying, recording, or by any information storage and retrieval system, without prior written permission from the publisher.

First edition 1997. Second edition 1999. Third edition 2000. Fourth edition 2001. Fifth edition 2005, reprinted with corrections 2009. Sixth edition April 2013, reprinted with updates 2017. Seventh edition 2020, reprinted 2022.

The National Center for Employee Ownership
(510) 208-1300
www.nceo.org

ISBN: 978-1-938220-87-6

Contents

Preface v

1. **A Primer on Leveraged ESOPs** 1
   Corey Rosen

2. **Understanding ESOP Valuation** 27
   Corey Rosen

3. **Section 1042 and the Tax-Deferred ESOP "Rollover"** 51
   Scott Rodrick

4. **Using ESOPs in Mergers and Acquisitions** 73
   William Merten and Vaughn Gordy

5. **Bank and Seller Financing for ESOP Transactions** 91
   David Solomon and Regina Carls

6. **Warrants in ESOP Transactions** 103
   Philip J. Carstens

7. **Alternative Financing Sources in ESOP Transactions** 117
   Dan Kaczmarek

   About the Authors 125

   About the NCEO 128

Preface

Leveraged ESOPs...

During the past several decades, employee stock ownership plans (ESOPs) have become a familiar feature on the U.S. business landscape. There are more than 6,600 companies with ESOPs; many of these ESOPs are leveraged, meaning that the ESOP has borrowed money on the credit of the employer or other related parties to buy company stock. It is the only qualified employee benefit plan that can do this. Moreover, the company can deduct ESOP contributions it makes for both principal and interest payments on the loan. This tax-advantaged leveraging capability, in conjunction with other tax advantages, makes the ESOP an ideal vehicle for several purposes, including buying a company from its owner(s); divesting a subsidiary, division, or product line from a larger company; enabling a public company to repurchase shares; restructuring existing benefit plans; and acquiring capital with a low-cost loan.

...and Employee Buyouts

A leveraged ESOP can be the ideal vehicle for an employee-led buyout. Thousands of companies have been established through selling a company to an ESOP or through corporate divestitures to newly created companies that are at least partially ESOP-owned. If a broad-based group of employees buys out a company or division, they will probably use a leveraged ESOP to do it. Hence, although there is no chapter in this book titled "Employee Buyouts," every chapter concerns issues to consider in an ESOP-based employee buyout.

About This Book

ESOPs are complicated mechanisms, and using leverage increases their complexity. This book is designed to be a practical tool for anyone dealing with that complexity, whether the leveraged ESOP will purchase a small amount of stock or be used for an employee buyout of part or all of a company. Business owners, managers, their advisors, lenders, and others interested in employee ownership plans will all find this book helpful. It covers not only financing, accounting, and other aspects of the transaction but also the rules for the tax-deferred "rollover" for a selling owner in a closely held C corporation under Section 1042 of the Internal Revenue Code.

About the Seventh Edition

The first edition of *Leveraged ESOPs and Employee Buyouts* appeared in 1997. In the seventh edition (2020), the book has been revised from the bottom up to be a more updated, streamlined, and practical guide for readers. A few chapters were kept but revised, and everything else was replaced with new material.

Chapter 1

A Primer on Leveraged ESOPs

Corey Rosen

When the owners of Barclay Water Management wanted to sell their shares in 2010 in the now 88-year-old company, they could have sold them to a competitor or a private equity firm. But that just did not feel right. The employees built the company and sustained its award-winning culture. Over the years, Barclay had allowed employees to buy shares in the company, and a number of them did, but the company had grown and there was no way employees could come up with the after-tax dollars needed to buy out the principal shareholders (who were also employees). At a conference in Chicago, CEO Bill Brett and I met. I described how an ESOP worked. Bill quickly concluded this was the way to go.

Soon after, Barclay set up an employee stock ownership plan (ESOP) and got a loan to buy 30% of the shares in the company from those ready to sell. Hitting that target allowed the sellers to have the option of deferring tax on the gains they had made on the sale by investing in stocks and bonds of U.S. operating companies. The loan was repaid by the company in tax-deductible dollars. Six years later, the ESOP used a loan from a bank and notes from the sellers to buy the remaining shares and make Barclay 100% ESOP-owned. It then converted to S corporation status and no longer had to pay income tax. Employees became the owners of the company through a trust under the ESOP without having to pay any of their own money. Today, even amidst the economic crisis, Barclay has grown and prospered.

Sellers got a fair price for the shares based on an outside appraisal. The employees got ownership they would earn through their future work. Sellers and the company got significant tax benefits. As owners, the employees have found new ways to help the company succeed. This all may sound too "just right," and, for some companies, an ESOP is not the right approach to transition, but for everyone at Barclay, it was a great success.

Owners of closely held companies like Barclay who want to sell their businesses to employees face a problem. The employees might be willing, but their wallets are probably not. Buying shares in a company is an expensive and risky proposition, and it all must be done in after-tax dollars. Selling to a competitor or a private equity firm may be an option, but only 10% to 20% of these buyers will offer any kind of premium over what an ESOP would pay. In many cases, these buyers, especially private equity firms, may want to reduce employment to increase short-term profits or eliminate duplication that results from a merger. Many will not retain the culture the company has built. Sellers have to sell the whole company all at once, even if they might prefer a more gradual exit. Sellers will have limited or no control over any ongoing role they have in the company. ESOPs are a very attractive way for the right companies to create a transition that, like Barclay's, provides flexibility, a fair price, tax benefits, and the ability to retain people and values. For most owners I talk to about ESOPs, as appealing as the financial benefits are, the real appeal is the legacy an ESOP creates.

So just how does an ESOP accomplish this? A simple solution is for the company to set up the ESOP trust and make discretionary annual cash contributions to the plan to buy shares from sellers. This gradual transition can work very well for many companies. But for most companies, sellers are older and looking to sell all or a part of their shares more quickly, and for this, they need leverage. This book provides a roadmap to how this works.

ESOPs started in the 1950s on a case-by-case IRS approval basis, and then became part of the Employee Retirement Income Security Act of 1974 (ERISA). ESOPs were specifically created to make it possible for ordinary employees to become owners of their companies through an employer-sponsored trust that receives corporate contributions of stock or cash to buy stock. ESOPs also were given the right, unique among employee benefit plans, to borrow money to buy company shares, money the company repays out of future deductible contributions. Most of the time, these ESOP loans are for business transition purposes, but companies can and do also use the borrowing capacity of ESOPs to buy other assets (including other companies) using pretax dollars, as well as for other corporate finance purposes.

ESOPs have borrowed hundreds of billions of dollars to buy stock in their companies since 1974. The simple idea behind ESOPs is that if Congress provided tax incentives to owners of existing businesses to provide collateral to back up ESOP loans, either by pledging corporate or personal assets, business owners would be more likely to share ownership with their employees.

In return for the substantial tax benefits this book describes for ESOPs, Congress insisted on some rules. "ESOPs must be fair," it decreed, creating a set of rules to define just what "fair" means. What follows here is an introduction to all these benefits and rules. Complex as they can be, however, the core concept is simple: ESOPs are a way to use the future earnings of the corporation to acquire ownership for employees. Tax benefits and, hopefully, the employees themselves help provide the added economic value to generate these additional earnings. In return for the tax benefits, companies must comply with rules designed to make sure the plans are rigorous enough to really provide benefits to employees, but not so rigorous that no company would set them up. The complexity of the laws is something that can easily be handled by professional advisors; people in companies just need to know the essential outlines.

What Is an ESOP?

An ESOP is a kind of employee benefit plan. ESOPs were given a specific statutory framework in 1974 with the enactment of ERISA and were the subject of new legislation, mostly to add benefits, in almost every Congress between 1974 and 1986, with some additional laws since then. Like other tax-qualified deferred compensation plans under Section 401(a) of the Internal Revenue Code (the "Code"), such as profit sharing plans and pensions, ESOPs must be operated for "the exclusive benefit of plan participants." This does not mean exactly what it says, though. It does not mean that other people cannot benefit from ESOPs, because no one would set them up were that the case. It does mean that when the interests of the participants of the plan conflict with the interests of people outside the plan, the participants should be paramount. Moreover, ESOPs must be operated by a trustee in a manner that is prudent and in compliance with the fiduciary rules of ERISA. Buying stock in the ESOP's sponsor when you, as trustee, know the company is about to encounter severe problems, for instance, is not prudent. Finally, ESOPs, like other qualified deferred compensation plans, must not discriminate in their operations in favor of highly compensated employees, officers, and owners. As was said of the Golden Rule, "all the rest is commentary."

Technically, an ESOP is a stock bonus plan qualified to borrow money. Whereas stock bonus plans are only required to distribute their benefits in the form of employer securities but can hold any mix of investments they like while people are still in the plan, ESOPs are required to invest primarily in employer stock. While there is no regulation about what "primarily" means, most ESOP specialists think it is over 50%. The percentage probably can temporarily drop below that from time to time, perhaps even for a year or two, and the rest of the assets can be invested in any sound investments. ESOPs can also start off by just receiving cash contributions from the company that are intended to buy stock later. Again, there is no consensus on how long an ESOP can do this, but doing it for two or three years seems safe.

How Leveraged ESOPs Work

Essentially, a leveraged ESOP is an intermediary in a loan transaction. Rather than borrow the money directly, a company borrows money and reloans it to an ESOP.

The company first sets up an employee stock ownership trust. The trust then borrows money to acquire stock in the company. The stock can be shares already owned, treasury shares, or new shares issued specifically for sale to the ESOP. Proceeds from the loan can be used for any legitimate business purpose. The stock is put into a "suspense account," where it is released to employee accounts as the loan is repaid. After employees leave the company or retire, the company distributes the stock in their account, which it must offer to repurchase at fair market value if the company is closely held. In the typical ESOP transaction, the lender will loan to the company, which reloans the money to the ESOP. Provided certain rules are followed, this "inside" loan does not have to be on the same terms as the "outside" loan. Lenders prefer loaning directly to the company, but the accounting and tax effects of this two-step process are essentially the same as if the loan were made directly to the ESOP.

In return for agreeing to borrow through the ESOP, the company receives significant tax benefits, provided it follows the rules to assure employees are treated fairly. First, the company can deduct the entire loan contribution it makes to the ESOP, within certain payroll-based limits described below. That means the company, in effect, can deduct interest and principal on the loan, not just interest. Second, the company, if a C corporation, can deduct dividends paid on the shares acquired with the proceeds of the loan that are used to repay the loan itself (in other words, the earnings of the stock being acquired help pay for stock itself). Again, there are limits, as described below in sections on the rules of the loan and contribution limits. Sellers to qualifying ESOPs in C corporations can defer capital gains taxes on the sale. While S corporations do not get this same tax benefit, any profits attributable to the ESOP are not subject to federal and, almost always, state income tax. Thus, whereas an S corporation normally pays distributions to shareholders to fund their tax bills, a 100% ESOP-owned S corporation generally has no tax bills to fund because the ESOP is not taxed.

Leveraged financing for an ESOP can come from banks, seller notes, and/or non-bank specialized financing. Banks have been very willing to loan to ESOPs if provided adequate collateral, while sellers can also take back a note and earn a competitive rate of interest. In a small number of cases, ESOP may also seek more specialized third-party financing, such as mezzanine debt or equity investors.

Uses of Leveraged ESOPs

An ESOP can borrow money for any business purpose. The most common of these is to buy out shares of an existing owner in a closely held C corporation. Under Section 1042 of the Code, a company can set up an ESOP and have it borrow money to buy shares from an existing owner. If the ESOP owns at least 30% of the shares in the company after that transaction, that sale, plus any subsequent sales, qualifies the seller to reinvest the proceeds in securities of U.S. operating companies and defer tax on the gain made from the sale to the ESOP until these replacement investments are sold. This tax benefit applies only to closely held C corporations; the seller must be an individual, an estate, one of certain trusts, a partnership, or an S corporation. Shares must have been held for at least three years (if the ownership form changes, such as from a partnership to an S corporation, the ownership of the shares in the new entity "tacks" onto the shares of the old one).

While this is the most common application of a leveraged ESOP, it is only one of several potential uses. For instance, an ESOP can be used to buy another company, an increasingly common application. Because contributions to the ESOP to repay the loan are tax-deductible, the acquisition can be made in pretax dollars. In this application, a company can, for instance, print new shares or issue treasury shares to sell to an ESOP, which borrows money to acquire them. Then the company uses the loan proceeds to purchase the target and repays the loan with tax-deductible contributions to the ESOP. Alternatively, the acquiring company could do a tax-free stock-for-stock merger with the target. Then the ESOP could borrow money to buy out the shares (now shares of the acquiring company) from the owners of the target. The acquirer can also finance the establishment of an ESOP in the target, which buys the owner's shares. Then the two ESOPs are merged and the target company dissolved. If both companies are closely held C corporations, as explained in the chapter on mergers and acquisitions, it is possible to structure this transaction so that if it meets the rules for the tax-deferred rollover described above, the seller or sellers can qualify for a tax deferral of gains on the sale.

Another application for a leveraged ESOP is to acquire new capital. Any ESOP, whether in a C or S corporation, or a public or closely held corporation, can use an ESOP this way. Here, the company issues new shares or treasury shares and sells them to the ESOP, which borrows the funds to acquire the stock. The sale proceeds then are used to acquire new machinery, buildings, inventory, or any other property that might otherwise be financed. The company can then repay the loan through the ESOP in pretax dollars. Of course, this will have the impact of diluting other shareholders, but it also provides an employee benefit at the same time it is financing growth more efficiently. A similar approach can be used to refinance debt. Public companies also use leveraged ESOPs to buy back shares from the market.

ESOPs are used in divestitures of subsidiaries. Here, a new acquisition corporation is established. It sets up an ESOP for the employees of the entity being sold. The acquisition company ("Newco") then borrows money, which it reloans to the ESOP, to enable the ESOP to buy newly issued shares in Newco. Newco uses the money from the sale to buy assets for the parent and then repays the ESOP loan out of future revenues.

In all these transactions, it is possible and sometimes necessary to combine the ESOP purchase with equity investments from managers, outsiders, or even the employees themselves. These investments do not count as ESOP ownership, however, when calculating tax benefits. For instance, if an ESOP buys 30% of a company and managers 20%, the seller in a C corporation can defer taxes only of the sale of the 30% to the ESOP.

Finally, leveraged ESOPs are often done in stages so that the company does not have the burden of repaying excessive debt all at once.

Setting Up a Leveraged ESOP

The Trust

Setting up a leveraged ESOP raises several issues. First, what is a trust? Generally speaking, a trust is an arrangement whereby property is transferred to a "trustee" who administers it for the benefit of a designated beneficiary. In particular, an ESOP trust is a legal entity that holds property, mainly company stock contributed by the employer or bought with funds contributed by the employer, for the ESOP's participants. Like other trusts, the ESOP trust is designed to protect its beneficiaries. A trustee is appointed to do this. The ESOP trustee must ensure that the shares are valued properly, must vote the shares (often based on directions from the board or an ESOP committee, but some companies have independent trustees and others allow employees to direct the trustees), must ensure that employee accounts are properly maintained, and must otherwise attend to the rules of ESOPs and the plan document.

To help assure independence, many ESOP companies appoint bank trust departments or other trust companies to serve this function. Other companies appoint managers or other insiders as trustees. The law does not prohibit insiders from acting as trustees, despite their potential conflict of interest. If a conflict should arise, however, and the ESOP, the company's board, and other at-risk parties are brought to court, the presence of an independent trustee may weigh in the company's favor. The Department of Labor, which along with the IRS is the coprimary regulatory agency for ESOPs, strongly favors outside trustees for any transaction between sellers and the ESOP trust, and our view at the NCEO is that companies are well advised to use this approach.

Who Lenders Can Be

Just about anyone can lend the ESOP money, including commercial lenders, sellers, and the company itself. ESOPs can also issue bonds to raise money, although this has been rare in recent years and is limited to the largest transactions. When a "party-in-interest" such as the seller or the company makes a loan, the terms of the loan must be not less favorable than an arm's length transaction (that is, similar to what might be available from a commercial lender facing comparable risks).

When a seller lends to an ESOP, this can be in an installment sale. If the company is a C corporation and the ESOP ends up with at least 30% of the company's stock, the seller can still qualify for one of the main benefits of an ESOP, the ability to defer taxation on gains made from the sale by reinvesting in qualified replacement investments. Only amounts reinvested during the period from 3 months before to 12 months after the sale qualify, however. The sellers cannot simply keep reinvesting and rolling over their installment payments. The seller can reinvest an amount up to the entire value of the sale, however, by using other funds. One popular approach addresses this problem by allowing sellers to buy long-term bonds with the loan proceeds. A broker would sell bonds equal in value to the note; the seller would use the first installment of the note as a down payment and borrow the rest from a bank using the bond as collateral.

Seller financing has become very popular in recent years. Sellers can structure the notes at rates similar to what a commercial lender would charge. In some cases, sellers also take warrants (the right to purchase a certain number of shares at the price the ESOP pays but for some number of years into the future) in return for lower interest rates. Companies buy back the warrants before they expire so the seller does not end up with stock again. Either way, the seller gets a rate of return on the note that is likely to be more than what other investments would yield and gets the principal purchased over time as well.

How the Money Is Borrowed

In the simplest form, the ESOP borrows the money directly, then uses it to buy company shares. The company then makes contributions to the ESOP to repay the loan. The ESOP may pledge the stock as collateral, but the company almost always must guarantee the loan with something more persuasive (assets or earnings). In addition, in many cases where the seller is reinvesting in qualified replacement property, the lender asks for part or all of these securities as collateral. Generally, as the loan is repaid, that portion of the collateral is released.

In practice, most loans are actually made to the company, which relends the money to the ESOP on the same or similar terms. Most lenders (including sellers) prefer to lend to the company. That way, they have better access to collateral and the company's cash flow, and fewer potential legal conflicts. The company can, however, make its loan to the ESOP on different terms than its loan from the lender, provided the transaction is an arm's length equivalent and the new terms of the loan to the ESOP meet fiduciary concerns (this is described in more detail below).

What Company Stock Can Be Used

ESOP rules are very strict on what qualifies as company stock. In closely held companies, the ESOP loan can only acquire stock with the highest combination of voting and dividend rights, or preferred stock readily convertible into such stock. In practice, that means ESOPs acquire either voting common stock or convertible preferred stock. In public companies, the ESOP can acquire any kind of common stock that is publicly traded. While the shares almost always must be voting shares, who votes them and how is more complex than it seems (it is not necessarily the employees). This is discussed in detail below.

In using preferred shares, it is important to make sure that the capitalization structure is not unfavorable to employee interests. Preferred shares whose upside potential is capped in value, for instance, are not considered in the employees' best interest. Preferred stock also must be structured carefully to assure that the conversion premium (the difference between the price of the preferred and the price of the common) is reasonable at the time the shares are issued.

Some companies have faced a problem when they issue dividend-paying stock to employees and find that under state laws they must pay the same dividends to holders of this stock outside the plan. This problem can be remedied, however, by changing the non-ESOP shares into some kind of non-dividend paying security beforehand.

The Rules of the Loan

A loan to an ESOP must meet several requirements. The loan must be at a reasonable interest rate, and only the stock in the ESOP acquired with the proceeds of the loan can be used as collateral (although the company or seller can, and almost invariably does, make its own guarantee with the lender). Only the dividends of the shares in the plan (called distributions in S corporations), contributions from the employer to repay the loan, and earnings from other investments in the trust contributed by the employer can be used to repay the loan. This means that dividends paid on shares acquired by the ESOP outside of the loan cannot be used to repay the loan, nor can the ESOP normally sell off shares in the trust to repay the loan unless the plan is terminated or the company is sold. In that case, all unpaid-for shares can be sold to repay the loan, with any amounts remaining after the sale being allocated to employees.

The loan must be without recourse to the ESOP, and must be for a specified term. The interest rate can be variable or fixed. There is no limit on the term of the loan to the company other than what lenders will accept (normally 5 to 10 years). Because the loan is usually made to the company and then reloaned to the ESOP, however, these bank-imposed limits do not necessarily limit the term of the company-to-ESOP loan. Provided the company can show that extending the term benefits employees, the term of the company-to-ESOP loan can be longer. For instance, extending the term of the loan to fit within the annual contribution limits would clearly benefit employees because, without such an extension, the plan would be disqualified. Extending the term to keep benefit levels more constant over a longer term might also qualify provided the benefit levels are significant.

Shares in the plan must be held in a suspense account. As the loan is repaid, these shares are released to the accounts of plan participants. The release must follow one of two formulas. The simplest is that the percentage of shares released equals the percentage of principal paid, either that year or during whatever shorter repayment period is used. In these cases, however, the release cannot be slower than what normal amortization schedules would provide for a 10-year loan with level payments of principal and interest. The principal-only method usually has the effect of releasing fewer shares to participants in the early years.

Alternatively, the company can release shares based on the percentage remaining in the account based on principal and interest paid. To do this the company divides the principal and interest payment it makes by the sum of (1) the principal and interest it still needs to pay and (2) the principal and interest it paid already that year. Stated more simply, the company bases its release on the total amount of principal and interest it pays rather than on the amount of the principal it repays. ESOP loans with a term of over 10 years must use this principal-plus-interest approach.

In either case, it is important to remember that the dollar value of the shares released each year is rarely the same as the amount contributed to repay the loan. If the price of the shares goes up, the amount allocated will be higher, in dollar terms, than the amount contributed; if they go down, the dollar value of the amount released will be lower. The amount *contributed to repay principal* is what counts for determining whether the company is within the limits for contributions allowed each year.

Refinancing ESOP Loans

Companies can refinance an existing non-ESOP loan with an ESOP loan under the same rules as if the loan were a new one. If a loan is refinanced, the shares are still allocated based on their original purchase price. Companies can refinance a loan that is reloaned to an ESOP without restriction because that transaction is between the company and the lender. ESOP loans themselves can also be refinanced under limited circumstances. Generally, a company wants to extend the existing term of the loan. In some cases, this is done because the company's payroll has shrunk, and the existing term requires payments that are above the contribution limits. In other cases, the company needs to repay the loan more slowly because of cash flow problems. The Department of Labor (DOL) has approved such refinancings. However, some companies want to refinance because their stock value has risen quickly, and they believe they are delivering "too much" value to employees. The DOL is much less favorable toward these refinancings.

Buying Back Unallocated Shares

Shares that have not yet been paid for are held in suspense before being allocated when loan payments are made. Some companies want to buy these shares back from the ESOP, often because they see them as a good value or because managers want to own more shares. In general, regulatory bodies frown on this because it denies employees an implied future benefit. Such repurchases are approved only in unusual circumstances. Note that this scenario is different from an outside purchase of all ESOP shares. That can be done if the ESOP trustee deems the sale to be in the best interests of plan participants.

Limitations on Contributions

Contributions to the Plan as a Whole

Congress was generous in providing tax benefits for ESOPs, but there are limits. Under Code Section 404, a C or an S corporation can contribute and deduct up to 25% of the total eligible payroll of plan participants to cover the principal portion of the loan, plus contributions to pay interest on the loan. In C corporations, contributions to fund the interest payments on the debt do not count toward the 25%-of-pay limit, but in S corporations they do.

Eligible pay is currently defined as pay not exceeding $290,000 per year (as of 2021; this figure is indexed annually for inflation, rounding in $5,000 increments). Note that eligible pay only includes people actually in the plan. In many "Section 1042" transactions, sellers, 25% shareholders, and certain relatives of these individuals are not included in the plan, nor are most new employees and others not yet eligible to participate.

In addition, dividends paid on shares acquired by the ESOP loan in a C corporation can be used to repay the loan, and these are not included in the 25%-of-pay calculations. Dividends used to repay a loan must release additional shares (from the suspense account if there are enough; from other corporate shares if not) to employee accounts with a value equal to the dividends. If employees leave the company before they have a fully vested right to their shares, their forfeitures, which are allocated to everyone else, are not counted in the percentage limitations. Theoretically, total payments made to the ESOP to repay a loan do not have to be adjusted downward because of other benefit contributions, but limits on how much individuals can get usually make this irrelevant. Employee deferrals to a 401(k) plan now count as eligible pay.

IRS private letter rulings have clarified that in C corporations (but not in S corporations), the 25% limit for deductible contributions to repay principal is *in addition* to contributions to other defined contribution plans, rather than being combined with them.[1]

Annual Allocations to the Accounts of Individual Participants

In evaluating limitations on contributions, it is important to understand that in addition to the deductible contribution limits based on the total amount of pay of plan participants as described above, there are limits under Code Section 415 on the amounts that can be allocated to any individual account in a given year (called the "annual addition" limits).

First, no one ESOP participant's account can receive more than 100% of pay in any year from principal payments on the loan, or more than $58,000 (as of 2021; this figure is adjusted annually for inflation in $1,000 increments), whichever is less. Contributions that do not meet these limits are forfeited and reallocated to other plan participants.

Second, the limits include company contributions to other defined contribution plans. Employee contributions to benefit plans are also counted toward this 100% of pay or $58,000 (as of 2021) figure.

Third, the interest is excludable from the annual addition limits for C corporations only if not more than one-third of the benefits are allocated to highly compensated employees, as defined by Code Section 414(q). If the one-third rule is not met, forfeitures are also counted in determining how much an employee is getting each year. In S corporations, interest always counts. Once an ESOP loan is repaid, forfeitures must count toward the annual addition limits.

---

1. See, e.g., PLR 200732028 (2007).

In calculating the annual addition limits for a leveraged ESOP that is repaying a loan, the dollar amount of the contributions used to repay the loan is generally counted as the annual addition, not the actual value of the shares that are released from the suspense account to a participant's account. For example, if the value of the company's stock has increased since the ESOP transaction, a $50,000 allocation to a participant's account will be used by the ESOP to repay the loan and release shares worth more than $50,000 into the participant's account.[2]

The effect of these provisions is that companies must very carefully assess just how much they can afford to borrow through the ESOP. Plans that violate these rules can suffer severe penalties, including plan disqualification. If payroll is inadequate, however, companies do have alternatives. The initial loan can be for less than the amount optimally desired, with a successor loan paying the rest. It may be possible to negotiate a longer loan period in order to stretch out contributions. Finally, and most importantly, companies can use dividends to repay the loan.

Using Dividends to Repay the Loan

C corporations (but not S corporations) can take a tax deduction when using dividend payments to repay the ESOP loan. These payments are not included in any of the calculations described above. Dividends on both allocated and unallocated shares are normally used to repay the loan. The dividends must be "reasonable." While this term has never been defined, most consultants believe it is a percentage of share value consistent with what other companies in the industry would pay given similar levels of profits. The dividends also must not be so high as to provide employees with "unreasonably" high compensation. The payment of excessive dividends will cause the dividends to be taxed, although it is not certain whether only the excess dividends or the entire dividend will be taxed. In extreme cases, the plan can be disqualified. Nonetheless, some very profitable companies can use dividends to increase the percentage of pay going to an ESOP to 50% or more.

A few companies use preferred stock in their ESOPs to allow for higher dividend payments. Whatever kind of stock is used, the amount

---

2. Alternatively, the plan may provide that the lesser of (1) the contributions used to repay the loan or (2) the actual value of the shares is used. Treas. Reg. § 1.415(c)-1(f)(2)(ii).

of the dividends must be allocated to employee accounts. Companies normally allocate these amounts in the form of shares released from the suspense account. For dividends paid on allocated shares and used to repay the loan, the value of the shares released must be at least equal to the amount of dividends used. That means that allocations of these shares to employees will be equal to the ratio of their account balance to the prior total amount in the plan. Dividends on unallocated shares that are used to repay the loan can be allocated on this same basis, on the basis of relative compensation, or according to some more equal formula. The allocation must occur in the year the dividend is used to repay the loan.

Using Distributions in S Corporations to Repay the Loan

Most non-ESOP S corporations make distributions of part of their earnings, usually to help owners pay their taxes. In an ESOP-owned S corporation, distributions received by the ESOP on both allocated and unallocated shares can be used to repay the ESOP loan (as well as for other purposes, including to repurchase shares or simply add diversity to employee accounts). Distributions paid on unallocated shares can release shares from the suspense account based on either the company's normal allocation formula (often a percentage of eligible pay), or based on the relative percentage of shares already allocated to a participant's account. For shares that have already been allocated from the suspense account, the distributions must release shares from the suspense account based on relative account balances.

Other Issues

The rules for leveraged ESOPs are similar to the rules of other qualified plans in terms of participation, allocation, vesting, and distribution, but several special considerations apply.

Who Must Be Included

All employees over 21 who work for more than 1,000 hours in a plan year must be included in the plan unless they are covered by a collective bargaining unit, are in a separate line of business of at least 50 employees not covered by the ESOP, or fall into one of several anti-discrimination exemptions not commonly used by leveraged ESOPs. If there is a union, the company must bargain in good faith with it over inclusion in the plan if the union wants to discuss the issue. Companies may want to include union employees in leveraged plans to maximize the amount of eligible payroll. If the ESOP does not replace other benefits, this normally can be done without requiring a reopening of the contract.

Allocations to Employee Accounts

As shares are released from the suspense account, they are allocated to individual employee accounts. This allocation can be on the basis of relative compensation (generally, all W-2 compensation is counted), but a more equal formula can also be used, such as per capita or seniority, or some combination. These other formulas must be written in such a way, however, that no highly compensated individual gets more than would be allocated under a relative pay formula.

If a more level formula is used, note that a formula that serves as an allocation cap (such as ignoring pay over $80,000 per year when allocating by relative compensation) can effectively reduce the level of eligible payroll. The company can only make deductible contributions that it can allocate, so if it cannot allocate as much due to a formula that caps allocations at a certain level, it cannot contribute as much. In some cases, this may mean there is insufficient eligible payroll to amortize the loan through the ESOP.

Vesting Rules

The allocated shares are subject to vesting. Employees must be 100% vested after three years of service (cliff vesting), or the company can use a graduated vesting schedule not slower than 20% after two years and 20% per year more until 100% is reached after six years. If the ESOP contribution is designated as a match to employee 401(k) deferrals (whether the ESOP and 401(k) are integrated or not), and the match is used to meet the "safe harbor" anti-discrimination rules for 401(k) plans, the contributions must vest immediately. Generally, if a company contributes 3% or more to the accounts of all eligible 401(k) participants (whether they make deferrals or not) or matches at a rate of at least 100%

for the first 3% of pay employees defer, and 50% for the next 2%, then it does not have to test for participation in the 401(k) plan.

Diversification

When employees reach age 55 and have 10 years of participation in the plan, the company must either give them the option of diversifying 25% of their account balances among at least three other investment alternatives or must simply pay the amount out to the employees. This option extends for each of the next four years. The diversification limit applies to the total share value in the participant's account (not the total account balance, part of which may already be diversified). If a participant chooses to diversify part or all of the eligible 25% in any year, an additional amount in each subsequent year can be diversified so that the total amount of shares diversified is 25%. Thus, an employee could diversify 25% of subsequent stock allocations, but could not diversify 25% of the total allocations in year one, then 25% of what is left in the account year two, etc. (this incorrect approach would result in over 75% diversification in year five). In the sixth year, eligible employees can increase their diversification to 50%.

Distribution Rules

Under the rules governing ESOPs, when employees retire, die, or are disabled, the company must distribute their vested shares to them not later than the last day of the plan year following the year of their departure. For employees leaving before reaching retirement age, distribution must begin not later than the last day of the sixth plan year following their year of separation from service. Payments can be in substantially equal installments over five years or in a lump sum. In the installment method, a company normally pays out a portion of the stock from the trust each year. The value of the stock may go up or down over that time, of course. In a lump-sum distribution, the company buys the shares at their current value but can make the purchase in installments over five years as long as it provides adequate security and reasonable interest. If a distribution is over $1,165,000 (as of 2021), the five-year period can be extended by one year for each additional $230,000 (as of 2021), up to five additional years (these amounts are indexed yearly). Distributions are generally made in stock or cash, but the participant has the right to demand shares. ESOP shares must be valued at least annually by an independent outside appraiser unless the shares are publicly traded.

There are two important exceptions to these requirements. If a company's charter or bylaws state that all or substantially all of the company's stock must be held by employees (inside or outside the ESOP), or the company is an S corporation, the company can require the employees to take the cash value of the stock. Second, C corporation leveraged ESOPs can delay the start of repayment until the loan is repaid, although exceptionally long delays (typically over 10 years) to start distributions are not recommended by ESOP advisors because they can make repurchase obligations unmanageable and damage employee morale. Note that the law does not specifically provide that S corporations can also delay payment until after a loan is repaid. Advisors generally agree that this was a technical oversight in the law and that the IRS would not object to a plan document including this provision (and we have no indication that they have yet done so).

The delayed distribution rules apply only to the shares acquired by the loan, not to all shares in the plan. For employees who terminate before death, retirement, or disability, the rules are relatively straightforward. Distributions do not have to start until the plan year following the plan year in which the loan is repaid. Distribution must be completed in the plan year following the plan year in which the loan is repaid or, if later, the date distribution would have to be completed under the normal distribution rules specified in the plan document and/or distribution policy. If a participant leaves in 2021, for instance, and the loan is repaid in 2023, the participant could still have to wait until 2027 to get a distribution, provided the plan and/or distribution policy provides that distributions do not have to start until five plan years after the end of the plan year the participant terminates.

There are also general qualified plan rules that apply to all aspects of distributions from retirement plans, including ESOPs, that can trump these ESOP-specific rules. Generally, the ESOP-specific rules will be the ones that are relevant, but the general rules state that distribution must start no later than the 60th day after the end of the plan year in which the later of these events occur: (1) the participant reaches age 65 or, if earlier, the plan's normal retirement age; (2) the 10th anniversary of participation in the plan; or (3) termination of service. These provisions can create somewhat complex interactions, as when an employee quits before retirement and after 10 years of service, and shortly thereafter reaches retirement age; at that point the general rules require distributions to begin, instead of waiting for the sixth plan year after the employee quits under the ESOP rules.

As with all retirement plans, distributions for any more-than-5% owners must begin no later than April 1 following the calendar year in which a participant reaches age 72, and distributions for other employees must begin no later than April 1 following the later of (1) the calendar year in which the participant reaches age 72 and (2) the calendar year in which the participant retires.

Finally, private companies and some thinly traded public companies must repurchase the shares from departing employees at their fair market value, as determined by the appraiser. This so-called "put option" can be exercised by the employee in one of two 60-day periods, one starting when the employee receives the distribution and the second period one year after that. The employee can choose which one to use. This obligation should be considered at the outset of the ESOP process and factored into the company's ability to repay the loan.

Within these limits, as long as a company does not discriminate between employees, it can set its own distribution requirements. A commonly recommended best practice is to write the maximum allowable distribution schedules into the plan but provide that a written distribution policy may provide more flexibility on a nondiscriminatory basis (the NCEO has model distribution policies in the issue brief *ESOP Distribution Policies*).

Voting Rules

Voting is one of the most controversial and least understood of ESOP issues. The trustee of the ESOP actually votes the ESOP shares. The question is "who directs the trustee?" The trustee can make the decision independently, although that is very rare. Alternatively, management, the board, or the ESOP administrative committee can direct the trustee, or the trustee can follow employee directions.

In private companies, employees must be able to direct the trustee as to the voting of shares *allocated* to their accounts on several key issues, including closing, sale, liquidation, recapitalization, and other issues having to do with the basic structure of the company. These general rules may differ in how they apply to specific cases, however. In public companies, employees must be able to vote on all issues. Private companies have the option of passing through voting rights on a one-person, one-vote basis.

Voting rights are more complicated than they seem, however. First, voting is not the same as tendering shares. So while employees may be required to vote on all issues, they may have no say about whether shares are tendered. In public companies, this is a major issue. Almost all public companies now write their plans to give employees the right to direct the tendering, as well as voting, of their shares, for reasons explained below.

Second, employees need not be given the right to direct the voting of unallocated shares. In a leveraged ESOP, this means that for the first several years of the loan, the trustee can vote the majority of the shares, if that is what the company wants to do. The company could provide that unallocated shares, as well as any allocated shares for which the trustee has not received instructions, should be voted or tendered in proportion to the allocated shares for which directions were received.

Third, if employees vote their shares on all issues, a company can still restrict their voting rights. The major issue on which employees would vote, of course, is who sits on the board of directors. A company could amend its bylaws to restrict who can be nominated for the board, thus retaining control within a management group, if desired.

The concern with voting rights may be more smoke than fire, however. Research by the NCEO indicates that employees are very conservative shareholders who normally support existing management. In a recent Gallup poll, 56% to 71% of people surveyed said if they were employee-owners, they would prefer to let management make decisions on a variety of corporate issues. Managers of companies that are employee-owned and employee-controlled say that employee voting rights have made very little difference in how their companies actually run. Of course, there are always exceptions, and these can cause legitimate management concern.

Unlike private companies, public companies usually want employees to direct the voting and tendering of shares. That is because trustees in an ESOP may see their role as maximizing the share value of the plan's holdings, thus causing them to accept an offer by an unwanted suitor. Employees, however, will probably (but not always) vote against a raider. In a key court decision, a Delaware judge ruled that if employees can independently direct the voting and tendering of the shares, an ESOP may be an effective defense against a takeover. There are many other considerations here, however.

Military Leave

In the case of employees on military leave, employers must comply with the Uniformed Services Employment and Reemployment Rights Act (USERRA). By law, for all retirement plan benefits, employees must continue to receive vesting as if they still worked for the company. There is no break in service. Employers are not required to make contributions or allocate forfeitures during the time of service, however. If there is a 401(k) plan, the employee has the right, over the lesser of five years or three times the length of employment, to make make-up contributions, and the employer would have to match these according to the formula that otherwise would have applied.

Accounting and Reporting Issues

The debt acquired by the ESOP must be counted as corporate debt, even if the corporation is able to get the loan without guaranteeing it. Until the late 1980s, banks often could obtain unguaranteed loans for their ESOPs and use the ESOP purchase of their shares to increase their capital, but this is no longer an acceptable accounting practice.

The offsetting debit to the liability recorded by the employer should show up as a reduction in shareholder equity (it appears as a contra equity account). The argument here is that the shares in the ESOP are held by a third party but are not yet paid for. As the loan is repaid and shares are released, both the liability and the offsetting contra equity account are reduced.

Amounts contributed or committed to be contributed to the ESOP need to be reported, with contributions to cover principal charged to compensation expense and interest accounted for as it normally would be allocated. Shares held by the ESOP are deemed as outstanding for calculations of earnings per share. For plans started after January 1, 1993, the value of shares released is their current market value. Plans started before then can use the acquisition cost or market value. Dividends should be charged to retained earnings except when dividends are used to repay a loan. Then they are charged to retained earnings for allocated shares and current earnings for unallocated shares. Where the principal-only method of repaying the loan is used, it may be necessary to take a charge to earnings equivalent to what the principal and interest method would produce.

These guidelines are based on the position of the American Institute of Certified Public Accountants (AICPA). Most were adopted by the Financial Accounting Standards Board in 1989. They are not laws or regulations, but standard accepted practices. Some accountants differ on one or more of these points.

Issues for S Corporations

Since January 1, 1998, S corporations have been able to have an ESOP own stock in the company. ESOPs are exempted from the unrelated business income tax (UBIT) that other nontaxable owners of S corporation shares are required to pay on their share on corporate profits. In other words, whatever percentage of the company the ESOP owns would not be subject to any current taxation. On the other hand, S corporation ESOPs do not have the same tax benefits available to C corporation ESOPs. Specifically, (1) owners of S corporation stock cannot use the tax-deferred Section 1042 rollover when selling to an ESOP, (2) dividends (i.e., S corporation "distributions") used to repay a loan or passed through to participants are not deductible, and (3) interest payments on an ESOP loan count toward the contribution limits.

There are complex rules to prevent abuses of the nontaxability of an S corporation ESOP's ownership interest. The good news for the large majority of S corporation ESOPs is that this will not affect them in any way. It will, however, prevent ESOPs from being used in S corporations to benefit just a few usually highly paid people. Specifically, the law defines certain ESOP participants as "disqualified persons." These are individuals who own 10% or more of the shares in the ESOP, counting allocated shares, their pro-rata share of unallocated shares, and, outside the ESOP, any stock options or other synthetic equity (this includes, among other things, a variety of kinds of deferred compensation). Direct ownership does not count. They also include people who, using family attribution rules, own 20% or more of the shares this way. If these individuals collectively own 50% or more of the company, including their ownership of synthetic equity, direct ownership, and ESOP ownership, then there is a 50% excise tax on the company, and allocations and account accruals to the disqualified individual are taxed as ordinary income. "Accruals" in this case means additions to plan participant accounts or to anyone who is a disqualified person under the rule even if he or she is not a plan participant. Accruals include additions to accounts from any source, not just allocations from company contributions. For instance, if unvested shares are reallocated within the plan, that would count as an accrual, as would additional shares bought within the plan from cash distributions. Violations can also occur if the number of shares changes. In short, anything that brings the disqualified persons over 50% ownership triggers the draconian taxes the law entails.

Another consideration for S corporation ESOPs concerns the payment of distributions. If the company makes distributions to any shareholders, it must make pro-rata distributions to the ESOP as well. So if a $1 million distribution is made in an S corporation 30% owned by its ESOP, the ESOP gets $300,000. This money can be used to repay a loan or just be added to employee accounts to create a cash balance in the plan that can be used to buy back shares in the future or for other purposes. While this can be very beneficial for S corporations with ESOPs (this is money that would have otherwise been used to pay taxes that now can be used for other purposes), as ESOP ownership percentages grow, the distribution amounts can be extremely large, creating in the process equally large employee accounts and, in some cases, violations of ESOP rules stating that the assets must be primarily held in employer securities. It also means that those with shares get richer and richer, while new employees get far less.

It is common for S corporations to convert to C status before setting up an ESOP so that sellers can take advantage of the Section 1042 rules that allow the deferral of gains on sales to qualifying ESOPs. S corporations doing that cannot reconvert to S status for five years. It is even more common for C corporations to convert to S status when they become 100% ESOP-owned. This conversion almost always makes financial sense, but there are some issues that need to be considered:

1. If a company uses LIFO (last in, first out) accounting procedures, there is an immediate recapture over four years of any excess inventory (not assets) with LIFO over what would have been the case with FIFO (first in, first out).
2. Built-in gains are taxable when assets are sold in C corporations. When they convert to S status, any gains on property sold within 10 years of conversion are taxable as income.
3. If a company has passive investment income for more than 25% of its income, then after conversion there may be an additional tax in excess of this. If income stays at this level for three consecutive years, then the company would lose its S status.
4. Certain tax benefits of being a C corporation, such as net operating losses, capital loss carryovers, and minimum tax credit from the AMT, cannot be carried over after electing S status.
5. S companies can only have one class of stock.
6. Interest payments count in calculating the contribution limits for the ESOP. Forfeitures of unvested shares that are reallocated also count toward the ESOP individual annual account addition limits.
7. Very small companies (less than 15 employees) may have a very hard time meeting the S corporation anti-abuse tests even if they have very standard or even egalitarian approaches to allocations.
8. In some cases, the ESOP deductions will be large enough so that the C corporation effectively has little or no tax anyway.

Valuation Issues

A separate chapter in this book deals with valuation concerns, but a few should be noted here. The fact of leveraging the ESOP may decrease the value of the shares because of the new debt, but not necessarily on a dollar-for-dollar basis. Valuation involves more issues than just the book value of the company, and these may provide additional value even after a 100% buyout. Although the company would have no net asset value after such a transaction, it still would have the capacity to earn income, and this provides some level of value. Second, the valuation should reflect the ongoing repurchase obligation. If it does not, then the shares will be overpriced; the obligation is a legal one and a very real liability to the company.

Should You Undertake a Leveraged ESOP?

Obviously, leveraged ESOPs are complicated and carry many obligations and restrictions. Their benefits are also substantial, however. So how does a company decide whether an ESOP is worthwhile, or, given that, whether a leveraged or nonleveraged ESOP would be more advantageous?

Before deciding on a leveraged ESOP, it is worth considering a nonleveraged ESOP. Some companies may not have the ability to obtain or repay a loan, or they may simply be averse to debt. In other cases, the company may not want to be constrained by a debt repayment schedule, instead preferring to make periodic discretionary cash or stock contributions to the ESOP. This means shares will be bought out more slowly, but if they are bought from existing owners, this may be acceptable if the owners are not in any rush to sell or think the stock price will rise over time.

A primary reason for using leverage is to enable the ESOP to acquire enough stock (30% of the company) to qualify sellers for the tax deferral of Section 1042. Some companies do this by accumulating cash contributions in the ESOP until there is enough to meet this goal (as noted above, this generally can be done for a few years), or putting in some cash, then borrowing the rest.

If an ESOP is used to borrow money, several issues need to be considered. First, companies need to consider any dilution effects the ESOP may create if the company is issuing new stock to the plan, rather than buying back existing shares. Most ESOPs do not issue new shares, however.

Second, companies need to evaluate carefully what the tax benefits of the plan will be (remember that all these benefits have no value to unprofitable corporations) and whether they will have adequate cash flow to service the debt. This may seem obvious, but in several cases, leveraged ESOPs have been used to buy out an owner, leaving the employees with more debt than they could handle, and their companies have closed.

Third, alternative forms of financing should be considered. The long-term benefits of an ESOP are hotly debated by experts solely concerned with their corporate financial impact. Equity or even straight debt may be preferable in some cases. That is especially the case when companies seriously consider (as too many do not) the repurchase obligation. ESOPs have up-front cash flow benefits, but require a long-term liability.

Fourth, public companies must consider the impact of the ESOP on shareholder relations. Leveraged ESOPs can make their financial reports look worse, unless offset by changes in other benefit plans. Yet these changes may have an undesired impact on employee morale.

Fifth, the size of the payroll relative to the size of the ESOP must be considered. ESOPs may simply not work in some companies because their total compensation is too small. While some companies may expect growth to solve the problem, lenders may take a more skeptical look at just how likely growth really is. For some companies, the answer to this may be a nonleveraged ESOP. This allows much greater flexibility in determining when and if to make contributions. The company can contribute as little or as much as it wants within applicable limits, however. This means, of course, that shares will be acquired more gradually, rather than bought all at once with a loan repaid over several years.

Finally, in any ESOP, but especially in one where the financial commitment is as fixed as a leveraged plan, ESOPs should never be installed solely because their tax benefits look appealing. Unless managers and owners are comfortable with and committed to the concept of employee ownership, an ESOP is not a good choice. Other financing and benefit plans offer tax breaks of their own. What ESOPs do is allow companies to share ownership with employees at the same time that they are financing other corporate objectives. But if a company is concerned only with the latter issue, and regrets the requirement of the former, eventually the ESOP will be seen as a mistake. ESOPs work best when companies share information, communicate about the plan regularly, and get employee owners more involved in the day-to-day decisions affecting their work. Absent these efforts, an ESOP is just another benefit plan and may not be the best one for any of the parties involved.

Chapter 2

Understanding ESOP Valuation

Corey Rosen

Why Do You Need a Valuation?

There is a T-shirt in the Exploratorium museum in San Francisco with a picture of Albert Einstein in a police hat. The legend on the T-shirt says "186,000 miles per second. It's not just a good idea, it's the law." If you want to have an ESOP in a closely held company, an independent, outside valuation is not just a good idea, it's the law. You must have an appraiser figure out what a willing buyer would pay a willing seller, assuming both have all the relevant information they need to make the transaction. The law is designed to make sure that the ESOP does not pay more than fair market value when it buys shares from a non-ESOP participant shareholder and that ESOP participants are paid fair market value when selling their shares back to the ESOP or the company.

Congress created this requirement to make sure that ESOP trusts are operated for the benefit of participants. Buying shares from an owner at an inflated price puts the company at risk and benefits the owner's interest at the expense of the plan participants. Many people call us at the NCEO, saying "Why can't we just use book value?" or some other formula, or perhaps the price they got in an offer from another buyer. Book value is simple, but it usually understates the real worth of ownership in most businesses. Most businesses are worth some multiple of their expected future earnings—earnings that are generated not just by assets, but by such intangibles as reputation, expertise, contacts, innovative ideas and processes, etc.

Other owners say they know that in their industry, businesses sell for an average of x times earnings or some other multiple. But your business is not likely to be average. If in using a formula you come up with a value that is just a few percentage points higher or lower than a more accurate assessment of your company's value, the costs will be much greater than the cost of a valuation. For instance, if your formula is off 3%, and your value is $2 million, then the formula is either costing you (if it is too low) or the ESOP (if it is too high) $60,000, many times the cost of an independent appraiser.

In addition, you are not simply selling your company when an ESOP buys the stock. You are selling shares in the company, and that is an important distinction. For instance, if you are selling a minority interest, the price per share is lower than if you are selling a controlling interest, because control has value. Even if you are selling a controlling interest, shares can have a discount for lack of marketability.

Because of all these factors, only a qualified appraiser can determine the right number. To make sure that the appraiser is working for the interests of employees, the law requires that the appraiser be independent, and the U.S. Department of Labor (DOL) and the courts have argued the best way to assure that is for the appraiser to be hired by the ESOP trustee (not the board, the company, or the seller) and report to the trustee.

Business owners sometimes worry that this appraised price will not be what they think they deserve or can get elsewhere. If you have a truly synergistic buyer interested in your firm, this might be true, although even then contingencies placed on the sale and less favorable tax treatment can make a lower sale price to the ESOP still a better deal. Truly synergistic buyers, however, are far less common than sometimes thought and account for a distinct minority of sales.

An independent appraisal is also essential to convincing employees that an ESOP is a good thing for them. If they believe that the ESOP is overpaying for its shares—that it is just a clever way, for instance, for the owner to take money out of the company on a tax-preferred basis—then employees are going to be very skeptical about the plan.

An independent valuation can be also be critical if there are multiple owners. If one sells for too high or too low a price, an artificial benefit or cost is created for one party or the other. In many ESOPs, sales are done in stages. Too high a price in the first stage means the shares the seller continues to hold are worth less and the company may be put in unnecessary financial danger.

Finally, having an appraisal can be a useful business planning tool. After all, the appraiser's report, which typically runs 75 pages or so, is all about comparing your business both to other businesses and to other uses for the money invested in your company. It thus provides a detailed benchmark to determine how you are doing and what elements of your strategy can be changed to improve equity value.

Who Hires the Appraiser?

The appraiser is hired by and reports to the trustee of the plan, not the seller or the board. Most trustees do not want the seller even to see the valuation report; some do not want board members to see it either, although on an ongoing basis, boards do normally get the valuation report or at least a detailed summary because it is so critical to understanding the business. While in practice the appraisal fees are normally paid for by the company, it is important that the contractual relationship be between the trustee and the appraiser. Thus, the recommendations directed to "you" below about hiring an appraiser are addressed to the ESOP trustee, and in particular an internal trustee (i.e., a company employee or committee) as opposed to an external trustee whose business it is to know these matters.

The fact that the appraiser's client is the ESOP trust, no matter who actually writes the checks to cover the fees, has important implications. First, the letter of engagement should clearly specify that the appraiser is working for the ESOP. Second, it means the appraiser is not trying to find the highest price that can be justified or, as in some tax-oriented appraisals, the lowest. Third, it should remind everyone involved that the point of the appraisal is to protect the interests of the ESOP participants by ensuring the ESOP does not pay more than fair market value in any purchase from an outside seller and that employees are paid fair market value for company shares in their ESOP accounts.

Many business owners have confidence that the appraised value will be one they are willing to sell at, often because their motivation in selling to an ESOP is only partly financial and they believe the price will reasonably reflect what their business is worth. Some sellers want to get an idea about what the ESOP will pay before doing a deal, however, and they or the company may hire an appraisal firm to determine a value on the same basis an ESOP appraiser would. That same firm may also provide advice on deal structure (seller financing, warrants, bank debt, cash in the company, etc.). If the firm is a qualified ESOP appraiser, its number will usually be within about 10% of what the appraiser hired by the trustee will determine. It is important to understand, however, that this firm should not be the same firm the trustee hires because that represents too much of a conflict.

When Must an Appraisal Be Performed?

The appraisal must be done before any sale to the ESOP. After the plan is set up, the law requires appraisals to be done at least annually, but there may be circumstances that require a more frequent appraisal. The law also requires that ESOP transactions be conducted at the current fair market value as of the date of the transaction. In practice, it takes some time to complete the transaction after the appraisal comes in, but the price would be at the appraised number.

If the ESOP is buying shares from an owner or the company, for instance, it should try to time its purchase to coincide with the most recent appraisal as closely as possible. On an ongoing basis, in an ideal scenario all transactions related to plan distributions (such as a departing employee selling shares back to the company or the plan) occur at a specific annual date that is timed as closely as possible with the annual appraisal. In practice, what this usually means is that the appraiser provides a report on a regular schedule and the plan administrator closes the plan year as soon as possible after that. That window is usually within a few months but may be longer. Statements are then mailed to employees, and transactions are completed as soon as administratively possible following the closing.

For distributions to employees, however, plans can also state that distributions will occur as of the most recent appraisal, even though that could be up to one year old. If this is done consistently, it is normally acceptable unless there is reason to think there has been a very significant upward or downward movement in share price in the interim. In that case, the trustee may ask the appraiser for a "drop-down" letter to state that the most recent appraisal is still valid or, if this is not the case, suggest an update be performed.

Who Performs an Appraisal?

The law requires an independent, outside appraisal from someone who is customarily in the business of doing business appraisals. There has never been a precise definition of what "independent" is, however. Clearly, some people are excluded—your board, your attorney, your brother-in-law, your CFO, your CPA, or anyone else with a direct financial relationship with the company. But what about your CPA firm (but not the person doing your books), or the valuation advisor who is affiliated with your attorney? Many people argue that if your CPA firm is large and can establish a "firewall" separating its audit and valuation sections, then that is acceptable. Others contend that even this is risky. Similarly, some people say you can use firms affiliated with your advisers (such as a valuation firm that pays a fee to your attorney for referrals), but most experts would argue that is not a wise policy.

We at the NCEO strongly suggest that you pick a firm that has no other business relationship with your company than the appraisal itself. Almost all the lawsuits that result in major judgments involving ESOPs concern valuation. The law looks primarily to process, not results, in determining whether the appraisal was fair to the ESOP. An appraisal done by a truly independent, qualified firm establishes a degree of credibility not possible any other way. With any other firm, there is always the possibility that the appraisal was done with an eye toward getting or keeping the company's business for the other parts of the firm or the affiliated parties involved in other parts of the transaction. The costs will rarely be lower in using someone not truly independent, so it is best to err on the side of caution.

In the past, the decision on whether a valuation firm that has done work for the firm before the ESOP could be hired by the trustee was a matter of disagreement, but that has changed. The DOL has been very clear on this issue in recent years and is very skeptical of appraisers who have any other relationship with the company. Appraisal firms that have done work unrelated to the ESOP should be excluded. A more difficult issue is whether an appraisal firm that is hired to do a preliminary appraisal for ESOP purposes can be used for the full-scale ESOP appraisal for the ESOP transaction. A preliminary appraisal can help a company decide whether to do an ESOP and to plan for financing it. Tim Hauser, a deputy assistant secretary at the DOL, has argued that this is "road testing" the appraiser to see if a high enough price can be obtained, and says the DOL wants companies to use a different firm for the transaction than for the preliminary appraisal, one hired by the trustee. Using a separate firm adds somewhat to the cost, but it also means the preliminary appraisal may come to a somewhat different conclusion of value than would be obtained from the firm that will ultimately do the ESOP appraisal, albeit the difference is likely to be small. Given the litigation and/or DOL investigation risks of using an appraiser who has done work for the company or the seller, and the fact that ESOP valuation professionals usually come to very similar conclusions of value, we strongly recommend that the ESOP appraisal firm have no other existing or prior relationship with the seller or the company.

The other major issue in determining whether an appraiser is qualified is competence. Here there are two areas to evaluate. The first is general business appraisal competence. Anyone can be a business appraiser. No specific degree and no licensing procedure is required by states or other entities. The appraisal industry does try to be self-regulating, however.

There are a number of organizations, offering a wide variety of designations, that provide some kind of business appraisal certification. Among these are the American Society of Appraisers (ASA), the National Association of Certified Valuation Analysts (NACVA), the Institute of Business Appraisers (IBA), and the American Institute of Certified Public Accountants (AICPA). Each organization provides some kind of technical education program providing certification designations. There are so many designations now that they can become quite confusing. It is worth asking an appraiser what designations he or she has and what was required to obtain them, but making comparisons on designations alone may be difficult.

In addition to these qualifications, you should also look at experience, in-house training requirements for the firm, whether the appraiser has spoken or published on the subject, and, of course, references.

Business appraisal competence is not enough, however. As will become clear later, there are many ESOP-specific issues. These issues can have a dramatic impact on the final valuation. Your appraiser should be able to demonstrate specific experience and expertise in ESOPs. Ask for a list of ESOP clients and call them. Find out whether the appraiser belongs to the relevant professional organizations (the NCEO and the ESOP Association), regularly attends professional conferences on the subject, and has spoken or written on ESOP-specific issues. If the appraiser claims to have ESOP expertise but does not meet these criteria, look elsewhere.

How Do You Find a Good Appraiser?

As noted above, an appraiser may be chosen by the seller, board, or trustee for advice on what the ESOP might pay, as well as possibly on deal structure. The trustee will hire the appraiser for the ESOP. In both cases, the criteria for selection are the same, although an independent trustee who does ESOP work often will have a list of appraisers it works with.

Both the NCEO and the ESOP Association maintain lists of appraisers and other ESOP professionals that are available to members. Neither group endorses the people listed in the guides, but at least this provides assurance that the appraisers are involved in the relevant professional organizations. Most active ESOP appraisers will appear on both lists. Your other professional advisors usually will also have recommendations, and you should ask other ESOP companies whom they have used.

One issue to decide is whether to pick an appraiser from a large or small firm. Large firms typically have an appraisal reviewed by one or more other staff members and may have additional credibility should there be a legal challenge. Some small firms, however, have excellent reputations and also may provide for internal reviews. Generally, large firms charge more, but this is not always the case. While there is not a right or wrong answer here, size per se is probably not a critical issue when comparing firms of comparable price, competence, and compatibility.

In picking an appraiser, it is wise to interview at least two or three candidates. You will find that there are significant variations in price, experience, and appraisal philosophy. The first two are obvious things to look for, but the third may seem a little confusing. Why ask about philosophy?

Different ESOP appraisers have different approaches to key appraisal issues, such as discounts for lack of control or liquidity (these are discussed below), or in their general appraisal approach (such as whether they rely more on earnings multiples or on comparable companies). These will have a potentially significant effect on value. Initial assumptions tend to get locked into your ongoing ESOP appraisal. It will always arouse suspicion if, a few years after the first ESOP appraisal, you decide you are unhappy with the approach and choose someone else who comes in with a different set of assumptions. Your business won't have changed, but ESOP participants and the IRS may now see a very different appraisal number. At best, you have a serious communications problem; at worst, you have a lawsuit or problem with the government.

To head off such complications, the ESOP trustee or the person who will become the trustee should interview appraisers beforehand. If the ESOP trustee decides down the road that the appraisal is in some way potentially faulty, the best approach is to hire a third party to do a review of the appraisal report (but not redo the appraisal). This is fairly inexpensive. If the review is positive, then things can continue; if not, the trustee may seek some changes in approaches by the appraiser or decide to hire an alternative firm (but not the one doing the diagnostic).

These interviews must be designed to find out what approaches are going to be in the best long-term interest of the ESOP and its participants. The goal is not to find the appraiser who will come up with the highest price. Instead, the trustee should be looking to assure, as best as possible, that the appraisal will support the long-term viability of the plan and that the appraisal will use methodologies that are generally accepted by the appraisal community and the regulatory authorities. That means the price will not be so high as to endanger the company's ability to pay for it nor so low that the current sellers will not want to sell. The appraisal assumptions and procedures must also assure that future participant distributions will be at their proper value. The ultimate price must fit within the range of what reasonable appraisers could agree is not more than fair market value.

Admittedly, these are somewhat vague guidelines, but ESOP appraisal is an art, not a science. While the process cannot be exact, however, it can and must be informed. A careful discussion with the appraiser about these issues prior to engagement can avoid confusion and unhappiness down the line. Note, however, that the appraiser may (appropriately) say that an initial discussion does not provide enough information to make an assessment of which approaches will work best.

Is the Appraised Price the One the ESOP Pays?

Once the appraiser has provided a report saying what fair market value is, that is not the end of the story. Many people incorrectly assume that this is the price that the ESOP must pay. Instead, the law requires that the ESOP cannot pay *more* than this price when purchasing shares from a seller. Indeed, it is the responsibility of the ESOP trustee to negotiate the best price possible, which sometimes will be less than the appraised value.

This negotiation might take a number of tacks. In a few cases, the seller prefers to sell for a lower price, usually because of concerns about the ability of the ESOP to repay the loan or just because the owner wants to be generous. In others, the trustee argues that tax benefits to a seller to an ESOP should come partly back to the ESOP in the form of a lower price. It is the ESOP, after all, that justifies the lower price as a result of its tax advantages. In still other cases, the ESOP trustee is simply bargaining for a better deal and, given the lack of other options the seller may have, is able to exert some leverage.

These scenarios all envision using an ESOP to buy shares from an existing owner. Sometimes an ESOP acquires new shares, such as when it borrows money to purchase shares to help finance growth, or when it accepts contributions of shares. In these cases, the trustee has less negotiating leverage because the contributions to the ESOP are diluting other owners, not buying their shares. Still, the size of a loan might be such that a lower price is needed to fit within legal requirements, or owners may wish to add another bargain element for the ESOP.

In an ongoing ESOP, participant shares are always purchased at the appraised value. You cannot, for instance, offer to pay a participant a lower price for an earlier distribution.

Opinions on Deal Structure

In addition to providing a valuation, the appraisal firm might be asked by the trustee to opine on deal structure. A significant minority of ESOP transactions are financed by seller notes in part or in full. In their simplest form, these notes carry an interest rate, usually determined based on the level of risk of that loan compared to senior bank debt. Some seller notes, however, also have warrants. A warrant is the right for someone (here, the seller) to purchase x number of shares at y price (here, almost always the fair market value for the company, as determined by the ESOP appraisal) for z number of years. Sellers take a lower interest rate in return for this right. Conceptually, what is calculated here is the present value of the forgone reasonable rate of interest expressed as the present value of the option to buy shares at today's price for some years into the future.

Say that Louise and her advisors conclude that a fair interest rate is 8%. But Louise is willing to take 4%. The note is for seven years. Say that that means Louise is giving up a cumulative $1 million in interest as a result. That has a present value of about $750,000. Louise now can trade that for the right to buy a number of shares at the current appraised price equal to $750,000 for the next seven years. If they go up in value, Louise will have the company cash them in and make money; if they go down, they have no value.

Pricing warrants involves a lot of math and a lot of assumptions. The appraiser may be asked by the trustee to determine if the pricing is fair.

In a much smaller number of cases, the company will seek outside equity investors. Now the appraiser may be asked to determine whether the deal they are getting is fair relative to the deal the ESOP trust is getting.

What Does the Appraiser Need from You?

In preparing an appraisal report, the appraiser will need a lot of data from you. The more precise and well prepared these data are, the better (and possibly cheaper) the appraisal will be. The following list indicates the key items appraisers generally need, although there may be other things requested:

- Financial statements, typically for the last five to ten years, preferably audited (but many smaller companies will present only reviewed statements). Income statements, balance sheets, cash flow and capital statements, and any explanatory footnotes or other material are included.

- Budgets or projections
- List of subsidiaries, if any
- Leases and contracts
- Compensation schedules
- Prior appraisals
- Dividend history and expectations
- Legal documents
- Prior sales or offers
- Shareholder list
- ESOP documents
- Operational information, such as sales by customer, patents, departmental budgets, competitors, etc.

In addition to a review of these documents, the appraiser will want to interview management and possibly board members, suppliers, customers, advisors, or anyone else deemed to have critical information. One or more site visits will be arranged. During these interviews, any significant issues that could materially affect operations, such as a pending environmental liability, a new competitor, management changes, or a patent expiration, for instance, should be thoroughly discussed.

It is important that your financial forecasts be realistic and well-justified. Forecasts that are built from the bottom up, vetted by multiple people, and reconciled are better than those just made by the CEO or the CFO. Forecasts should be stress-tested for possible increases or decreases, and that information shared with the appraiser. Excessively optimistic forecasts underlying appraisals have been a key element in ESOP litigation.

What Is in the Appraisal Report?

Valuation reports typically run from 50 to 90 pages. The report will cover several issues. The basis for the appraisal of the company as an enterprise should be thoroughly explained and justified (for instance, if the appraiser chose to use an earnings ratio as a key element, why that was more appropriate in this case than some other methodology). Then there should be a discussion of any discounts or premiums applied to that value for the shares the ESOP is purchasing. Again, a thorough explanation of assumptions and rationale should appear. The data used for making the determination should be outlined, and any weightings or judgments used in assessing these data should be elaborated. Any special factors that affect valuation findings, such as a change in management that could reduce future value, should be covered. Reports usually also include a number of charts and tables showing different indications of value based on different methods.

In addition to these matters, the report should follow the guidelines included in the Department of Labor's proposed regulations concerning valuation. Among other things, these include a discussion of the business, its markets, and general economic considerations affecting value. The company's book value should be considered, along with any goodwill or other intangible assets and the company's dividend-paying history and capacity. The price of similar companies, if any, should be provided. Finally, issues relating to marketability and control concerns need to be reviewed. The trustee needs to show that the process for selecting an appraiser has been thorough and resulted in the selection of a legitimate ESOP valuation expert. The trustee must also show that the financials provided to the appraiser are accurate and realistic, not best-case scenarios. In ongoing valuations, the appraiser should be able to demonstrate how the repurchase obligation has been factored into the final price.

The final valuation will be a blending of these issues. Because there is no formula for valuations, however, each report will be different.

Steps in the Valuation Process: What Is Fair Market Value and How Is It Calculated?

In calculating how much the ESOP can pay, the first step is to determine how much the business is worth as an entity. There are three basic approaches used to determine this: the asset approach, the market approach, and the income approach.

Asset Approach

This is the simplest approach and one many closely held companies already use to value their shares for purchases by key employees. It is also the least used method in ESOP appraisals. In this approach, a company is assessed based on either the liquidation value of its assets or its adjusted book value. The adjusted net asset methodology approach takes the balance sheet and transforms it from an accounting document to an economic one. For instance, an asset may be fully depreciated on the balance sheet, but still have resale value on the market. Liabilities may not appear on the balance sheet because they are contingent, such as a possible environmental issue (cleaning up a landfill, for instance). Inventories also need to be adjusted for what they could currently sell for in the market. Any accounts receivable and payable not on the balance sheet need to be considered. Any intangible, but marketable, assets (such as a trade name) need to be assessed.

While these methods are simple, they are also usually wrong. People usually want to buy a business because it can yield them a return on their investment; the ESOP always looks at a purchase this way. While a company's assets are part of what creates an income stream in a company, they are only part of it. All sorts of other factors—expertise, reputation, contacts, processes, labor practices, and other issues—condition how much a company can make. The asset approach has even less relevance when only a minority stake is being sold because minority owners cannot force a liquidation of assets.

There are a few companies, however, where the asset approach may show up as one of the weighted factors. You may also see asset value added back into the final calculation of value where there are assets that could be liquidated in a way that would have a positive effect on cash flows, or are worth materially more than the reported amounts on the balance sheet. For instance, if you own a building that has substantial value in a high-cost neighborhood, but could relocate to a lower-cost area without damaging cash flow, that extra value may be added back to the final value. That could also be true for cash on the balance sheet in excess of projected needs, more commonly measured as excess working capital. To the extent that cash (working capital) or other assets are "excess," i.e., not required to generate a given level of earnings, their market value will generally add to the value estimated through earnings measures.

Market Approach

The next approach is to see what, if any, evidence there is of how much people would pay for stock in the company or comparable companies. There may be, for instance, a history of stock sales in the company, or there could be other valid offers. These offers, however, do not necessarily establish a value that the ESOP can pay.

The market approach can use the guideline company method or the merger and acquisitions method. The guideline company method estimates the value of a business by comparing the subject company to publicly traded ownership interests in comparable, or guideline, companies. The merger and acquisition method is based on an estimate derived from the value of the sale of a controlling interest in comparable companies involved in mergers and acquisitions, most of which will be private firms, often sold for private equity investors. In either case, multiples of earnings paid by investors are used to create multiples that would apply to your company.

The methods have limitations. The offers in the M&A data are for control and possibly for synergistic control. As discussed below, control premiums in ESOPs, if they exist, are more nuanced than in these markets. If the offer is from another company with a synergistic interest in the target company, it is not a useful comparison because the ESOP valuation assumes a financial buyer. If International MegaCompany can gain operating efficiencies, or eliminate competition, by buying Pete's Pizza Parlors, they will pay more for Pete's than would a buyer who could not capture these efficiencies. The ESOP is always a *financial* buyer; it must be able to justify its purchase based on the return that investment yields as a stand-alone company, although heavy acquisition activity in a given industry may influence market pricing upward and should be considered.

Better data are available from public companies (the guideline company method), but here several complicating issues arise. First, many public companies have multiple lines of business. Second, they are almost always larger, and often much larger, than the company being appraised. Third, they may have very different capital structures than closely held companies. These and other differences make direct comparisons difficult. Most business appraisers are experienced in dealing with these complications, however, so the data on stock prices in these companies can yield useful insights about the typical ratios (such as share price to annual earnings) that can be applied, with appropriate adjustments, to provide benchmarks for applying multiples to the company being valued. When using public companies, the indicated value for the company being appraised is a minority interest, freely marketable value because the share prices of the publicly traded companies represent small minority interests in the public company.

However a market approach is constructed, a company's earnings may be "normalized" to reflect how another buyer would operate the business. This is discussed in more detail below in the section on the income approach to valuation.

Income Approach

A third set of methodologies falls under the income approach. The basic theory behind these methodologies is that a buyer is looking to make a reasonable return on an investment over an acceptable period of time, given the relative risk of the investment. A theoretical willing buyer is looking at a variety of investment choices. There are safe ones with low returns (CDs, T-bills, etc.), somewhat riskier ones with higher returns (stocks and bonds), and still riskier ones with the highest returns (individual companies). It has to be this way: the higher the risk, the greater the return an investor will demand. In buying a company, then, the investor needs to know two basic things: what the risk is and what the income flow is that will result from the investment. There are a number of ways to conceptualize these factors, but the two most common are referred to as capitalization of free cash flow and discounted cash flow.

Capitalization of free cash flow method: With the capitalization of free cash flow (FCF) method, the appraiser develops an estimate of the company's sustainable level of free cash flow. This is usually based on history and estimates of what future FCF will be. FCF is defined as follows:

      Net income
- `+` Non-cash charges (such as depreciation)
- `−` Increases in working capital
- `+` Additions to long-term debt
- `−` Payments of long-term debt
- `−` Capital expenditures
- `=` Free cash flow (FCF)

Free cash flow is normally used because that is the basis from which an investor can earn a return from the investment either in the form of dividends or investment of the FCF back into the business for future growth. However, some appraisers prefer other variations on the future income theme, such as earnings before interest, taxes, and depreciation.

After these numbers are determined, they are adjusted to reflect nonrecurring items and special considerations. For instance, there may have been a large one-time expense that lowered earnings (and thus FCF) in a prior year, or an anticipated one-time expense in the future projections. Very commonly the pay and perquisites of executives or other employees needs to be adjusted to reflect what the market rates for these individuals are, unless these practices will remain in place after the transaction. If the CEO is making $700,000 a year and has a company-paid vacation to France every year, the appraiser might determine that these expenses would be substantially reduced if someone else bought the company. This excess is added back to earnings if the levels of compensation will not continue into the future. Similar adjustments to earnings and cash flow are typically made before applying multiples in the market approaches as well. After analyzing historical and potential earnings, the appraiser will determine a single figure called "representative earnings."

Finally, a capitalization rate is applied to these representative cash flows. The concept here involves some complex math, but the basic idea is simple. The appraiser is trying to determine what the present value of a future stream of sustainable FCF is. The rate is derived by subtracting the expected long-run rate of FCF growth from the company's discount rate. The discount rate, in turn, reflects the rate of available risk-free investments and the risk adjustments appropriate for the fact that this is an equity investment made in a company of a certain size (there is less risk in a large company) with specific risk concerns.

For instance, an appraiser might determine that in a particular business, the expected FCF growth rate is 6% per year. The discount rate is 25%. The capitalization rate is now 19%, and this is divided into expected FCF to determine the company's value. If the next year's (or sustainable) FCF is $3 million, the company would be worth $3 million divided by .19, or $15.8 million before considering appropriate discounts or premiums. The underlying concept here is that the investor is looking to obtain a return on investment that justifies the risk. In this case, the return would be 19% on the expected annual FCF.

Discounted cash flow approach: A similar approach is the discounted cash flow method. Here the discount rate (25% in this case) is applied to a measure of FCF. Theoretically, all the earnings could be paid out this way to justify the investment, and this would provide a benchmark for determining value. Again, annualized free cash flows are determined; these are then discounted back to the present at the required rate of return or discount rate. The appraiser will add a terminal value at the end of the forecast period to complete the analysis.

The choice of method will depend on the degree to which past earnings are the best predict of future earnings. Discounted cash flow will be used when a good case can be made that the future forecasted earnings are more indicative of what the company will make.

The discount rate is determined by a weighted average cost of capital calculation. In simple terms, this is the rate of return the hypothetical buyer needs. The weighted average cost of capital is a way to look at the various components a buyer should think about in calculating that. The buyer would want to know what interest rates are (debt capital), what the yield is on equity investments (the cost of equity capital), how much the equity in the company is relative to equity plus debt, and the tax rate of the buyer, not the ESOP company. The buyer's tax rate may not be the same as the target company. That is especially true in an S corporation ESOP where part or all of the income is shielded from tax. The buyer cannot be presumed to be an S corporation ESOP but must, instead, be presumed to pay a normal corporate tax rate. That means the after-tax earnings of an S corporation will be reduced when applying the tax rate of the hypothetical buyer. In addition, a company risk factor is usually added of between 1% and 3% to reflect the additional return the buyer will need for investing in a company with this risk profile.

With either method, the value of each year's projected earnings over the next five years is progressively discounted, and the residual value of all future years after that is added. These out years become so highly discounted that they can be estimated as a lump sum. The total of these numbers is the enterprise value. Debt is subtracted from that, then divided by the number of shares. That value may be further adjusted for lack of control, lack of liquidity, and the repurchase obligation, as discussed below.

The discount rates vary over time and with a variety of factors. In recent years, discount rates of 12% to 20% have been common.

What Discounts or Premiums Apply to ESOP Value?

Whether or not any discounts and/or premiums apply to the indicated values derived using the valuation methods described above depends on numerous factors. In ESOP valuations, discounts generally fall into two categories: liquidity and control. These are discussed in more detail below. But before knowing whether to apply a discount, it first must be determined whether or not the valuation is being conducted on a controlling interest (or enterprise) basis or a minority interest basis. Then, depending on the method and data used within the valuation method, appropriate discounts and/or premiums are applied. Similarly, whether to apply a liquidity discount depends on whether the comparisons used to determine value are based on liquid or illiquid interests in companies.

Liquidity and Repurchase Obligation Issues

If you buy shares in IBM, you can sell them any time and get your money in three days. If you buy stock in Sally's Computers, there is no ready market for the shares. You might not be able to sell them for years, and you may have to settle for less than market price if you need the money and no one is eager to buy. This lack of marketability creates a discount over the price for the sale of otherwise comparable shares in a public company or shares in a closely held company about to be sold (because in this case there is immediate liquidity). So in any closely held company selling shares other than in a total sale, there is a discount over what the price would be for publicly traded shares, usually in the range of 20% to 40% depending on the circumstances, such as any restrictions on the sale of stock, buy-sell agreements, prospects of an initial public offering, dividends, or the availability of other buyers.

Many ESOP appraisers contend that the presence of the ESOP mitigates or even eliminates this discount. ESOP rules require that departing employees have the right to put their shares back to the company (or have the company fund the ESOP to do this) at fair market value. This seems to eliminate the lack of marketability.

The reality is more complicated, however. First, there must be some assurance that the company can really muster the cash to repurchase the shares. Second, the put option does not belong to the ESOP, for which the appraisal is being made, but the participants in the plan. Third, the put option applies only in a limited window of time and only when people leave the company or can diversify their accounts. That is hardly the equivalent to owning shares in a public company.

Appraisers argue back and forth on the legal and practical issues involved here. The typical discount for lack of marketability in an ESOP company, according to NCEO studies, is 5% to 10%.

In some appraisals, the liquidity discount is where the repurchase obligation is reflected. In that case, setting a liquidity discount should not simply consist of picking some round number that seems reasonable. The obligation of a company sponsoring an ESOP to buy back shares from departed ESOP participants represents a future use of nonproductive assets. This obligation means money is not available for other uses. If the company "recycles" the shares, either by contributing cash to the ESOP to buy the stock or by buying the stock directly and recontributing it to the ESOP immediately or over time, then the number of outstanding shares remains the same, while the discounted future cash flow per share declines by the magnitude of the obligation. This should produce an iterative set of calculations. The obligation will lower value, but the new lower value means a lower future obligation.

The calculations keep being repeated until a solution is found. The resulting number should be a precise one, just as other elements of the valuation are, not just a "best guess."

On the other hand, if the company redeems shares and does not recontribute them, then the number of shares drops proportionately to the decreased future cash flow, producing a neutral effect on share value but reducing enterprise value.

An emerging (and we think better) practice for the repurchase obligation, however, is to calculate the amount of the obligation over the coming years that is in excess of what the company would normally pay for benefits. This results in lower projected earnings. That results in a lower value, which makes the repurchase smaller, so the calculation is run again (and again and again in what is called an iterative process) until a solution is found. This calculation is affected by how much cash is in the ESOP, recycling versus redemption policies, and other factors.

In some cases, the ESOP trust already has considerable cash, often because the company is an S corporation and has an ESOP that has received ongoing distributions, or because the company has contributed cash in addition to stock. In effect, these transfers have already accounted for the repurchase obligation in lower earnings than otherwise would have been the case, so an additional discount is not needed.

Including the repurchase obligation in the valuation requires the appraiser to have a copy of a repurchase analysis. Companies that do not go through this process, and do not require the appraiser to factor it into the final result, will overpay for the shares, endangering the future ability of the company to grow or to honor its repurchase obligation.

Lack of Control (Minority Interest) Discounts and Control Premiums

In most ESOP valuations in the past (and some still today), a company with a minority ESOP would be valued with a discount for lack of control and would get a premium when the ESOP went over 50%. The value of this was largely a matter of judgment from the appraiser. That approach has changed, however, and, especially if you are a minority ESOP, you are likely to see a more complex and possibly mathematical calculation.

The ESOP community is adopting a firmer and simultaneously more nuanced position regarding the attributes and value of "control" in ESOP transactions and valuations. Under a more nuanced framework, the appraiser typically starts by determining a value for the enterprise as a whole based on the supposition that regardless of how much the ESOP owns, the company will endeavor to use its assets in a financially responsible and optimal way. The premise is similar to that applied to public companies, where there is rarely a singular controlling owner and the business is operated with the objective of maximizing shareholder outcomes. Executives and managers in public companies who fall short of achieving shareholder objectives on a standalone basis, whether due to suboptimal results or industry disruption (among other reasons), may find their businesses exposed to strategic events, including mergers, acquisitions, and/or divestitures, whereby the new or successor business is expected to provide superior investor outcomes that result primarily from enhanced cash flows. In contrast, if an industry player perceives opportunity in a business combination with a lesser and/or optimizable target, there will be strategic acquisitions aimed at enhancing value outcomes for all (i.e., 1 + 1 = 3). When these events occur and the underlying pre-transaction values are compared to the transaction values, there is almost universally a measurable value premium. Generally, this premium results from the expectation that cash flows and the resulting investor outcomes from a business combination will be superior to that of a standalone going concern, even under the presumption that the standalone enterprise is already reasonably optimized.

The increasing, if not consensus, view of the ESOP valuation community is that the use of control premiums in their legacy form and magnitude likely results in valuations that reflect efficiencies and/or synergies associated with strategic control value. In doing so, these valuations likely reflect value in excess of fair market value and are thus at risk for being labeled "prohibited transactions" using conventional ESOP regulatory interpretations. If an ESOP valuation contains explicit strategic treatments to cash flows or the implied equivalent by way of an excessive control premium, the value is likely overstated and potentially problematic for the transaction and/or the ESOP's future sustainability. While such synergies and efficiencies might be available in a marketplace of motivated investors, such treatments are not directly relevant to fair market value in the normal course of an ESOP company that remains an independent going concern on a standalone basis.

If a closely held ESOP company whose valuation begins with a financial control model for the company as a whole (or something constructively similar) has an ESOP that owns less than a controlling interest, then the valuation for ESOP purposes may require discounting to reflect the additional value captured in the underlying model. But the economics of control can get foggy and require nuanced understanding and careful consideration. For example, company bylaws may require a supermajority for certain decisions. So even a majority ESOP trustee may not have full control, and there could arguably be some potential discount for that, but not as much if the ESOP had no control rights at all.

Another critical issue is that the DOL has been skeptical about the argument that an ESOP trustee has full control even with supermajority or 100% ownership. For instance, if the seller is on the board, does that mean the seller retains some control? In itself, it probably does not, especially if the seller is no longer the CEO and there are outside board members. But what if the seller is the CEO and the majority of board members are his or her employees? Or what if the seller has covenants on the ESOP loan restricting the use of cash flow before a seller note is paid? These factors and others might lead to an analysis of partial control. The challenge of quantifying the effects of governance and differentiating values as a result of form over economic substance is not unique to ESOP valuations and quite frankly may never be fully resolved. The remedy for overcoming the questions surrounding control and its varying shades of gray is likely in the substance of the transaction terms and consideration, thus removing as many doubts as possible about the pro forma economics and cash flows that will affect the ESOP company's performance after an ESOP transaction.[1]

The Impact of Leverage on Valuation

If the ESOP borrows money, it will have an impact on valuation. The interest expense on the new debt the company now has taken on to fund the ESOP will show up on the balance sheet and, in any event,

---

1. Tim Lee of Mercer Capital contributed valuable editorial suggestions on this section.

represents a significant non-productive expense. While this generally will not reduce value dollar-for-dollar (there are ESOP tax benefits, the company may grow, and there is a discount for the future value of money), it will reduce the post-transaction value. This effect will disappear as the loan is repaid.

This impact is important for two reasons. First, employees need to understand why this drop occurs. Their own account values start at the lower value and thus are not reduced by the debt (unless the loan is to a previously existing plan), but they need to understand the issue to avoid communications problems. Other owners will also see their share price drop, of course. If they plan to sell before the ESOP loan is repaid, this could present a problem. In some cases, companies arrange for pro-rata sales from owners to avoid this issue.

S Corporation Issues

When the ESOP trustee receives a statement of the pro-rata share of earnings on which taxes would be paid each year, the trustee can ignore it. ESOPs do not have to pay tax on their share of the S corporation's earnings. Clearly, S status with an ESOP can enhance earnings, yet, just as clearly, a potential willing buyer would be unlikely to maintain the ESOP. So from that buyer's standpoint, the future earnings would be unaffected by this special tax benefit. As a result, the standard practice in ESOPs is to not "tax effect" the earnings. However, over time, the tax savings will help the company grow faster and more profitably.

Conclusion

The requirement to have an ESOP appraisal is designed to assure that the ESOP process is fair to all parties involved. While many business owners would prefer to set their own prices using a formula or a number derived from prior offers, these simplistic approaches rarely result in the price the ESOP would pay as a financial buyer. ESOP trustees, as well as owners, managers, and employees of ESOP companies, need to understand the valuation process well.

Chapter 3

Section 1042 and the Tax-Deferred ESOP "Rollover"

Scott Rodrick[1]

One of the main uses of an ESOP is to buy out the shareholders of a closely held company. An ESOP is ideally suited to that task for various reasons: for example, it provides a ready market for the selling shareholders' shares; shareholders can sell in stages instead of all at once; it preserves continuity at the company by not bringing in a third-party buyer who may disrupt operations (e.g., by firing people or selling off parts of the company); employees are given a new retirement plan that, in conjunction with a participative management approach, can produce notable performance gains; and the company receives tax deductions for its contributions to the ESOP.

But there is yet another factor that drives many ESOP transactions: the tax-deferred "ESOP rollover." Under Internal Revenue Code ("Code") Section 1042, the shareholders of a closely held C corporation can indefinitely postpone taxation on the gain resulting from the ESOP sale to the extent they reinvest ("roll over") the sale proceeds in securities of U.S. operating corporations. Nobody likes to pay taxes, even at the lower long-term capital gains rates, and the savings afforded by the "ESOP rollover" are a powerful incentive for prospective sellers to an

---

1. The author thanks David Solomon of Levenfeld Pearlstein, LLC, the coauthor of chapter 5, for his assistance in revising this chapter for the seventh edition of this book. James Steiker of SES ESOP Strategies; Michael Coffey of Corporate Capital Resources, LLC; and Keith Apton of UBS assisted in preparing a previous version of this chapter.

ESOP.[2] The tax laws in most states mirror Code Section 1042, so the tax-deferred rollover it provides is particularly valuable for sellers who live in states with higher personal tax rates.[3]

The Section 1042 Rules in Brief

Section 1042 was not originally part of the laws governing ESOPs. It was added to the Code by the Tax Reform Act of 1984.[4] The tax deferral afforded to a shareholder who sells their stock to an ESOP does not apply automatically, which means that the selling shareholder must affirmatively elect Section 1042 treatment.

This chapter will begin with a brief summary of the rules for the tax deferral and then follow with a more detailed discussion of each point. Most of these rules are contained in Section 1042 and other sections of the Code, but others are in temporary regulations promulgated by the Internal Revenue Service (IRS) in 1986. The main requirements for a sale of stock to an ESOP to qualify for the Section 1042 tax deferral are as follows:

- The company sponsoring the ESOP must be a closely held C corporation, not a publicly traded company or an S corporation.
- The ESOP must own at least 30% of the common equity of the company after the transaction.
- The selling shareholder cannot be a C corporation but rather must be an individual, trust, estate, partnership, or limited liability company (LLC), or perhaps an S corporation.

---

2. The tax-deferred "ESOP rollover" for the seller under Section 1042 should not be confused with the rollover of an ESOP distribution into an ESOP participant's IRA or other qualified benefit plan.
3. For example, California Revenue and Taxation Code Section 18042 specifies in part that "Section 1042 of the Internal Revenue Code, relating to sales of stock to employee stock ownership plans or certain cooperatives, shall apply to taxable years beginning on or after January 1, 1995."
4. Section 1042 applies not only to ESOPs but also to certain worker-owned cooperatives. This discussion will focus on ESOPs because this book is about ESOPs. Additionally, Section 1042 is almost always used for ESOPs.

Chapter 3: Section 1042 and the Tax-Deferred ESOP "Rollover" | 53

- The stock sold to the ESOP must have been held by the seller for at least three years before the sale. (When stock ownership is exchanged for a prior partnership or LLC interest, the total time of ownership is measured, as described below.)
- The stock sold to the ESOP must *not* have been acquired through a qualified retirement plan (such as an ESOP) or through a stock option or discounted employee stock purchase arrangement.
- The stock sold to the ESOP must be common stock with certain voting power and dividend rights, or preferred stock convertible into such common stock.
- During a period starting three months before the sale and ending a year after the sale, the seller must reinvest ("roll over") the proceeds or an equivalent sum of money (in any amount up to the amount of the sale) in "qualified replacement property" (QRP) (basically, the securities of U.S. operating companies).
- With certain exceptions, if the ESOP disposes of any of the stock within three years after the sale, the company must pay a 10% excise tax.
- For at least ten years after the sale, the ESOP must not allocate stock bought in the sale to the ESOP accounts of the seller or certain relatives of the seller. With no time limitation, the ESOP must not allocate such stock to any more-than-25% shareholders or to related parties of more-than-25% shareholders deemed to hold stock by attribution. Otherwise, the company must pay a 50% excise tax, and the person receiving the allocation is currently taxable on the value of the allocation.
- After the sale, the seller must file the following two documents with the seller's income tax return for the year in which the sale occurs:
    1. A "statement of election" under which the seller elects tax-deferred treatment.
    2. A verified statement from the company consenting to the imposition of the 10% and 50% excise taxes referred to above if the ESOP disposes of the stock within three years after the sale or makes a prohibited allocation.

Furthermore, every time the seller purchases QRP, the seller must obtain:

3. A notarized "statement of purchase," which then must be filed as discussed below. (If the QRP has been bought at the time of the Section 1042 election, the statement(s) of purchase must be filed along with the statement of election.)

The Section 1042 Rules in Detail

Nature of the ESOP Sponsor

Section 1042 applies only to sales to an ESOP established in a domestic C corporation.[5] For at least one year before and immediately after the sale, the company, and each corporation that is a member of the same controlled group of corporations with the company as defined in Code Section 409(l), must have no stock outstanding that is readily tradable on an established securities market.[6]

Shareholders selling to an ESOP in an S corporation cannot take advantage of Section 1042. An S corporation that wishes to make the Section 1042 "rollover" available to its shareholders may terminate its S corporation election, thus converting to C status.[7] A C corporation that is ready to adopt an ESOP and would like to elect S status may remain a C corporation long enough for the tax-deferred sale to the ESOP to take place, and then elect S status the year after the sale.

The 30% Requirement

Immediately after the sale, the ESOP must own at least 30% of either each class of outstanding stock or the total value of all outstanding stock (excluding in both cases nonconvertible, nonvoting preferred stock, but including stock constructively owned through options, warrants,

---

5. Code § 1042(c)(1)(A).
6. Ibid.; Code § 409(l); Temp. Treas. Reg. § 1.1042-1T, Q&A-1(b).
7. No delay is needed after termination of the S election. In PLR 200003014 (Oct. 20, 1999), the IRS ruled that a seller could undertake a Section 1042 sale immediately after the company changed from a S corporation to a C corporation.

or convertible debentures).[8] Section 1042 transactions are often accomplished through a sale of convertible preferred stock representing more than 30% of the *value* of all company stock but less than 30% of the outstanding common stock upon conversion. Note that the ESOP need not own any stock before the sale.

Sales to the ESOP by two or more shareholders can be treated as a single sale meeting the 30% requirement if they are "part of a single, integrated transaction under a prearranged agreement" between the sellers.[9]

Who Can Sell to the ESOP and Elect 1042 Treatment

Usually, the selling shareholders who elect Section 1042 are individuals. They also can be partnerships, trusts,[10] estates, or limited liability companies (LLCs). They cannot, however, be C corporations, and it is unclear whether they can be S corporations.[11] If the seller is a partnership or LLC, it is the partnership or LLC itself, not individual partners or members, that makes the Section 1042 election and purchases the QRP.[12]

---

8. Code § 1042(b)(2). Section 1042(b)(2) applies the attribution rules of Code Section 318(a)(4), under which someone with an option to acquire stock is treated as owning such stock. The term "option" in Section 318(a)(4) includes warrants and convertible debentures when they are redeemable at the election of the holder. Rev. Ruls. 68-601, 1968-2 C.B. 124, and 89-64, 1989-1 C.B. 91.

9. Temp. Treas. Reg. § 1.1042-1T, Q&A-2(b).

10. Section 1042(a)(1) specifies that the "taxpayer" elects 1042 treatment. A trust can sell to an ESOP and elect Section 1042 where it is the taxpayer (e.g., not a revocable grantor trust), as in PLR 9143013 (July 18, 1991). In PLR 200337003 (Sept. 12, 2003), where stock had been transferred to revocable grantor trusts and was to be sold to an ESOP, the "taxpayers" who could elect Section 1042 treatment and purchase QRP were the grantors, not the trusts.

11. Code § 1042(c)(7) (regarding C corporations). Section 1042 does not specifically exclude S corporations from acting as selling shareholders in this context. However, in 2001, during discussions leading to an ESOP-related private letter ruling, the IRS firmly rejected a suggestion by the ESOP practitioners requesting the PLR that an S corporation could sell to an ESOP and elect tax-deferred 1042 treatment. The practitioners then withdrew that issue from their PLR request. Also, it is unusual for an S corporation to own C corporation stock in the first place.

12. Technical Advice Memorandum 9508001 (Oct. 13, 1994) and PLR 9846005 (Nov. 13, 1998) (dealing with partnerships); PLR 200243001 (Oct. 25, 2002)

Nature of the Stock Sold in a 1042 Transaction

The stock sold to the ESOP must have been held by the seller for at least three years before the ESOP transaction, determined as of the time of the sale.[13]

To reach the three-year holding requirement, a seller who has held the stock for less than three years may take advantage of the "tacking" rules in Section 1223 of the Code. These rules allow the seller, in certain circumstances, to "tack" on the holding period of an asset that was exchanged for the stock in a transaction where both the stock and the asset for which it was exchanged have the same basis (i.e., a gift or tax-free exchange).[14]

The gain on the sale of stock sold to the ESOP must be otherwise eligible for long-term capital gain treatment, i.e., it cannot be stock that is ineligible for capital gain treatment, such as preferred stock subject to Code Section 306.

The stock sold to the ESOP must not have been acquired through a qualified retirement plan (such as an ESOP), through exercising stock options, or through restricted stock or discounted stock purchase arrangements under Section 83 of the Code.[15]

The stock sold to the ESOP must be (1) common stock having a combination of voting power and dividend rights equal to or in excess of (a) the class of common stock having the greatest voting power and (b) the class of common stock having the greatest dividend rights, or (2) preferred stock convertible into such common stock at a reasonable conversion price.[16] (Note: this is not a Section 1042 requirement but

---

(dealing with an LLC). Note: for federal tax purposes, an LLC is generally treated as a partnership.

13. Code § 1042(b)(4).
14. Douglas Jaques, "'Tacking' On to the Section 1042 Seller's Holding Period," *Journal of Employee Ownership Law and Finance* 8, no. 1 (winter 1996): 29.
15. Code § 1042(c)(1)(B). Although the statute is unclear on this point, many ESOP practitioners think that stock acquired at fair market value (or above) in an employee stock purchase arrangement should be eligible for Section 1042 sales. However, at least one IRS representative has informally stated that this is not the case and that absolutely no stock acquired through an employee stock purchase arrangement may be sold to an ESOP in a Section 1042 transaction.
16. Code §§ 1042(c)(1), 409(l).

Chapter 3: Section 1042 and the Tax-Deferred ESOP "Rollover" | 57

rather is a general requirement for most ESOP tax incentives applicable to closely held companies.)

Qualified Replacement Property (QRP)

To obtain the Section 1042 tax deferral, the seller must reinvest proceeds of the sale in QRP during a period beginning 3 months before and ending 12 months after the date of the sale, i.e., the date the stock is sold to the ESOP.[17] The tax deferral lasts as long as the seller holds the QRP (this is discussed more below).

QRP Need Not Be Bought with the Actual ESOP Sale Proceeds

The IRS does not trace the funds from the sale; as is apparent from the "3 months before" aspect of this rule, the actual funds from the sale need not be used. For example, a seller who has $1 million to invest can buy QRP three months before the ESOP transaction, receive $1 million in the transaction, and freely invest or spend the $1 million in proceeds from the actual sale.

The Seller Can Elect Section 1042 Treatment for Any Amount of the Proceeds

Also note that the seller can elect Section 1042 treatment for any amount of the sale proceeds. Of course, this means that the seller will pay capital gains taxes on the amount not reinvested under Section 1042. Thus, a selling shareholder might receive $1 million from an ESOP transaction, reinvest half of it in QRP and elect Section 1042 treatment for that amount, and spend the other half (or rather what remains of it after paying capital gains taxes) on the purchase of some other assets other than assets that qualify as QRP.

What QRP Can and Cannot Be

The QRP itself must consist of securities issued by a domestic operating corporation. "Securities" in this context includes stock; rights to subscribe for or to receive stock; and bonds, debentures, notes, certificates, or other evidence of indebtedness issued by a corporation, with interest coupons

---

17. Code § 1042(c)(3).

or in registered form.[18] A domestic corporation is one incorporated in the U.S.[19] Section 1042 defines an "operating corporation" as one where more than 50% of the company's assets were used in the active conduct of a business as of the time the security was purchased or before the end of the 15-month period for buying QRP. No more than 25% of the corporation's gross income can come from passive investment income.[20] However, shares in financial institutions defined as banks in Code Section 581 and in insurance companies subject to taxation are specifically designated as "operating companies" under Section 1042 and thus are excluded from the passive income rule.[21] Government securities cannot be QRP.[22] Real estate investment trusts (REITs) and partnership interests also are off-limits.

The rollover securities need to qualify as QRP only when the seller buys them and elects to treat them as QRP. If, for example, a seller buys a company's stock as QRP and a few years later the company becomes a non-operating company or reincorporates in a foreign country, the seller can keep holding the stock as QRP.

The QRP must consist of the actual securities themselves, not mutual funds.

There is no prohibition against reinvesting in securities of closely held companies, but the QRP cannot include securities of the ESOP company itself—that is, the company whose shares were sold to the ESOP (e.g., a shareholder in Company X cannot sell 30% of Company X's stock to Company X's new ESOP and then buy more Company X stock to serve as QRP). Corporations controlled by the ESOP company or that own stock representing control of the ESOP company are also excluded from being QRP.[23] However, it would be permissible for the QRP to consist of shares in another company owned by the seller that was not in the same controlled group of corporations, including a new corporation funded wholly with the ESOP sale proceeds.[24]

---

18. Code Sections 1042(c)(4)(D) and 165(g)(2).
19. This would include a U.S. subsidiary of a foreign corporation.
20. Code § 1042(c)(4)(A)-(B).
21. Code § 1042(c)(4)(B)(ii).
22. Code § 1042(c)(4)(D).
23. Code § 1042(c)(4)(C).
24. PLR 9720026 (Feb. 12, 1997).

Investing in Floating-Rate Notes (ESOP Notes) as QRP

One strategy that investment advisors have devised for clients who have elected 1042 treatment is to use floating-rate notes (sometimes called "ESOP notes") that are issued by large public companies. ESOP notes are structured to allow their holders to ensure compliance with the requirements of Section 1042. These are long-term highly rated corporate bonds, often with a maturity of 30 to 50 years, that pay an adjustable rate of interest pegged to short-term benchmark rates.[25] (When a bond matures, is called, or is sold, that constitutes a disposition of the QRP, which in turn triggers the capital gains taxes that the QRP investment was intended to delay in the first place.) The appeal of this investment is that the floating-rate notes theoretically have low credit risk and low interest rate risk and therefore can be used as collateral for borrowing at a very high ratio to their value. These ESOP notes usually come with both a put and call feature. The call feature is designed to eliminate the risk of the note being called away, which would create a disposition of the QRP, and the put feature allows the QRP investor to sell the note back to the issuer as needed at a specified price and date outlined in the prospectus.

The selling shareholder can often borrow 80% to 90% of the value of the ESOP Note and invest the borrowed sums freely while still deferring taxes on the original sale to the ESOP, which has considerable appeal for some individuals. However, there are costs involved to set up the transaction, and to benefit from this strategy, the investor must (after any brokerage and management fees) generate higher returns with the amount that was borrowed than the investor would with 100% of the sale proceeds invested in a conventional buy-and-hold QRP portfolio. Additionally, in a credit crisis a floating-rate note may lose much of its value (as happened in 2008 for QRP investors who had bought AIG notes), which could trigger a margin call, although after such a crisis the notes may regain their value. In the event of a margin call, the QRP investor might be forced to liquidate part of the QRP if the investor is unable to deposit the cash necessary to cure the margin call. This cash

---

25. At the time of this writing that is the London Interbank Offered Rate (LIBOR), which is scheduled to be phased out at the end of 2021 and replaced with the Secured Overnight Financing Rate (SOFR).

will be released back to the investor if the bond regains its value after the markets settle or its credit regains its footing. Should the investor be forced to liquidate part of the floating-rate note holdings, this would create a taxable event not for the full deferral, but for the portion of the QRP that was sold.

The possibility of a credit crisis makes the use of the ESOP notes questionable for seller-financed transactions where the shareholder lacks the assets to meet a margin call. Banks providing monetization loans secured by QRP have taken this into consideration since the 2008 financial crisis by requiring annual personal financial statements showing that the client has the means to meet a margin call should one occur. The risk of a margin call, however, can be minimized through creating a diverse portfolio of floating-rate notes instead of only using a single issuer.[26]

The floating-rate note QRP strategy is often recommended for older investors who will hold the notes until death and who have several million dollars or more to invest in QRP, are ready to deal with the costs and risks this strategy entails, and are willing to create a diverse portfolio of floating-rate notes from multiple issuers.[27] For such investors, the flexibility that the floating-rate note strategy provides can help mitigate risk in changing capital markets.

General QRP Investment Strategies

Selling shareholders should not feel compelled to follow a special investment strategy such as buying floating-rate notes and borrowing

---

26. As an illustration, after the collapse of Lehman Brothers in September 2008, the value of the AIG floating-rate note dropped to 70 cents per dollar. This created a margin call for many investors. For those that had a diversified portfolio this caused little harm, as the margin call was on a small percentage of the portfolio. For those that had a heavy concentration in financials, including AIG, this created a much greater problem, as the impact of the margin call was much larger. However, AIG did honor the put price of 98 cents on the dollar for many of the securities that individual floating-rate note investors held. The sale of the note back to AIG was a disposition of QRP and thus a taxable event, the impact of which was relatively small when the AIG floating-rate note was just a small part of a broad QRP portfolio.
27. For a more detailed discussion of floating-rate notes as QRP, see Christopher J. Clarkson and Stacie Jacobsen, "Investing After You Sell Your Business to an ESOP," in *Selling to an ESOP*, 11th ed. (NCEO, 2020).

against them. In many cases, sellers and their advisors conclude the best strategy is simply to invest in stocks and bonds that qualify as QRP and that would be good long-term investments regardless of their status as QRP. At any rate, sellers are advised to use qualified investment advisors to avoid traps such as investing in a seemingly eligible U.S. company that fails to qualify as QRP because it had too much passive income.

Donating the QRP to a Charitable Remainder Trust

The selling shareholder may invest the sale proceeds in QRP (thereby avoiding capital gains taxes) and then donate some or all of that QRP to a charitable remainder trust (CRT). In return, the shareholder receives a tax deduction plus annual income for the remainder of the shareholder's life, for the lives of the shareholder and his or her spouse, or for a fixed period. The gift is irrevocable, however, and thus the shareholder's heirs will not inherit the QRP. Another option is for the shareholder to avoid selling to the ESOP and instead contribute the stock to a CRT, which then may sell to the ESOP.[28]

When (and Whether) Tax Is Due Upon Disposition of QRP

As noted above, when the seller disposes of any QRP, the gain that was deferred is now realized, and the seller must pay taxes on the portion of the deferred gain that the sale represents.[29] The basis of the QRP is the basis the seller's stock had when it was sold to the ESOP.[30] However, no

---

28. For details, see Clarkson and Jacobsen, "Investing After You Sell Your Business to an ESOP," 118–20.
29. Code § 1042(e)(1).
30. Code § 1042(d). Literally, the taxpayer's basis in the QRP is reduced by the gain not recognized due to the 1042 election, so the basis of the stock sold to the ESOP becomes the basis of the QRP. This means that if the QRP loses value and is sold, the seller may still owe taxes. For example, say that the selling owner's basis in the stock is $200,000, and they sell it to the ESOP for its fair market value of $1 million. To avoid paying taxes on the $800,000 gain, the seller reinvests the $1 million in stocks of 10 companies at $100,000 each and elects Section 1042 treatment. Under Code Section 1042(d), the unrecognized gain of $800,000 reduces the seller's $1 million basis in the QRP to the $200,000 level of the stock sold to the ESOP, allocated pro-rata to each of the investments. Years later, the value of one of the $100,000 QRP investments has

gain is realized if the stock is exchanged for stock of another company in a tax-free corporate reorganization under Code Section 368, by reason of the seller's death, by gift (such as a charitable contribution, or a transfer to a charitable remainder trust or to the seller's relatives[31]), or in another transaction to which Section 1042 applies.[32] And if a seller holds QRP until dying, the heirs receive a basis in the QRP that is stepped-up to the fair market value of the stock at the time of death,[33] thus achieving a complete avoidance of taxation on the proceeds of the sale to the ESOP.

Some sellers have the misconception that holding QRP is like holding stock in a tax-deferred account such as an IRA, where dividends and interest on the assets held in the account are not taxable. This is not the case with QRP: the tax deferral applies only to the proceeds from the sale to the ESOP, and all earnings from the QRP are taxed.

Similarly, sellers should remember that tax is due only on the QRP that has been disposed of. Thus, a seller may elect Section 1042 and make small sales of QRP over time to rebalance his or her portfolio, paying the appropriate tax upon each disposition. Along the same lines, sellers should remember that even a short- or medium-term tax deferral may be useful in a given situation.

Using the QRP as Collateral

The section above on investing in floating-rate notes as QRP discusses using the notes as collateral for a loan to the *seller* so the seller can invest the borrowed money outside the constraints of Section 1042. In an entirely different context, some or all of the QRP can be pledged as collateral for a bank loan in the ESOP transaction itself.

---

fallen to $50,000, and the seller disposes of the stock. Although the seller lost half of the $100,000 investment in this portion of the QRP, its basis is $20,000 (i.e., its pro-rata portion of the $200,000 basis in the stock sold to the ESOP), and they now owe taxes on $30,000 (the difference between the $50,000 in proceeds from the sale of the QRP and the $20,000 basis of the QRP).

31. In PLR 201024005 (June 18, 2010), the IRS ruled that a selling shareholder's transfer of QRP to his spouse in connection with their divorce was not a disposition because it constituted a gift.
32. Code § 1042(e)(3).
33. Code § 1014.

The ESOP's Three-Year Holding Period

If the ESOP disposes of any stock within three years after the sale, the company must pay a 10% excise tax on the amount realized by the ESOP on the disposition. The IRS does not trace the particular shares that were sold. Rather, the law imposes the tax if, after the disposition in question, either (1) the total number of shares in the ESOP is now less than the total number that the ESOP held immediately after the sale, or (2) the value of the stock held by the ESOP is now less than 30% of the value of all employer securities as of the date of the disposition.[34]

The foregoing rule does not apply to an exchange of stock by the ESOP for stock of another corporation in certain tax-free reorganizations, or to benefit distributions due to termination of employment or in connection with ESOP diversification requirements.[35]

The Prohibited Allocation Rule

If the selling shareholder elects the Section 1042 tax deferral, the ESOP is prohibited from making allocations of stock from that transaction to the seller, more-than-25% shareholders, and certain relatives. If the company wishes to compensate key employees who are prohibited from receiving ESOP allocations under this rule, it cannot use a tax-qualified retirement plan meeting the requirements of Code Section 401(a) to allocate shares or other benefits in place of the prohibited ESOP shares.[36] Instead, the company must use plans such as stock options (including tax-qualified options), restricted stock, phantom stock, stock appreciation rights (SARs), and direct stock purchases.

Prohibition on Allocations to Sellers and Related Individuals

For a "nonallocation period" of the later of (1) 10 years after the sale or (2) after the allocation of stock attributable to the final loan repayment if it was a leveraged transaction, the ESOP cannot make allocations of

---

34. Code § 4978(a)-(b).
35. Code § 4978(d). To be precise, Section 4978(d) refers not to termination in general but specifically to distributions due to death, disability, retirement after age 59½, and separation from service resulting in a one-year break in service.
36. Code § 409(n)(1).

stock from the 1042 transaction to the selling shareholder and anyone related to the seller as defined by Code Section 267(b).[37] Among family members, such related individuals include only siblings, spouses, ancestors, and lineal descendants (including legally adopted children),[38] and thus do not include aunts and uncles, etc.

Other Section 1042 Sellers

The IRS held in a private letter ruling that where several people sold to the company's ESOP and elected Section 1042 treatment, and one was an ESOP participant (who was unrelated to the other sellers), that participant was prohibited from receiving any allocations of any ESOP shares, not just the ones he sold to the ESOP. The IRS stated that "none of the shareholders who sold . . . stock to the ESOP may receive an allocation . . . because [they] all . . . elected the application of [S]ection 1042(a)." The applicable "nonallocation period" was the one for selling shareholders as stated in the paragraph above (the later of 10 years or after the final stock allocation when the loan was repaid).[39] Any selling shareholder who will be employed by the company going forward should carefully consider the value of the Section 1042 election against the potential benefits to be realized under the ESOP as a participant if the selling shareholder avoids exclusion from the ESOP by forgoing the Section 1042 election.

Prohibition on Allocations to More-Than-25% Shareholders

So long as shares from the 1042 transaction remain in the ESOP, they cannot be allocated to more-than-25% shareholders (i.e., with no time limit). More than 25% means not just more than 25% of the entire company but also more than 25% of any class of stock, more than 25% of the *value* of any class of stock, or more than 25% of any class of stock (or the value of such stock) in a member of the same controlled group of corporations.[40] For purposes of determining the percentage

---

37. Code § 409(n)(1)(A) and (3)(C).
38. Code § 267(c)(4); Treas. Reg. § 1.267(c)-1(a)(4).
39. PLR 9041071 (July 18, 1990).
40. Code § 409(n)(1)(B).

of ownership, one must include stock owned by certain other parties and attributed under Code Section 318(a).[41] These parties include, for example, spouses, children (including legally adopted children), grandchildren, and parents, but other relatives such as grandparents are not included.[42] Additionally, stock allocated to the individual under the ESOP must be counted.[43] (This means that ESOP allocations could push a participant over the 25% threshold and make him or her ineligible for further allocations of shares from the Section 1042 transaction so long as the person is a more-than-25% shareholder.) When determining the percentage of ownership, one must also include stock that can be acquired under options, warrants, or conversion privileges for which there are no conditions that have not been met.[44]

It is important to note that under the attribution rules, someone may be a more-than-25% shareholder even if they are not usually thought of as being a shareholder at all. Thus, if someone owns 30% of the company, a son of that shareholder who works for the company will also be considered a more-than-25% shareholder and thus prohibited from receiving ESOP allocations of stock sold in the Section 1042 transaction. Another example is when someone owns more than 25% of a class of stock (and not necessarily anything close to more than 25% of the entire company) in another company that is a member of the same controlled group. The more-than-25% ownership test is applied to the entire one-year period ending with the date of sale to the ESOP, and also on the date that stock sold in the 1042 sale is allocated to ESOP participants.[45]

---

41. Code § 409(n)(1).
42. Code § 318(a)(1); Treas. Reg. § 1.318-2(b).
43. Code § 318(a)(2)(B)(i) (under Code § 409(n)(1), the employee trust exception in § 318(a)(2)(B)(i) is disregarded). The legislative history to Section 1042 clarifies this refers only to shares allocated to the participant's account (Explanation of Technical Corrections to the Tax Reform Act of 1984 and Other Recent Tax Legislation [Title XVIII of H.R. 3838, 99th Congress, Public 99-514], p. 155).
44. Code Section 318(a)(4), under which someone with an option to acquire stock is treated as owning such stock. The term "option" in Section 318(a)(4) includes warrants and convertible debentures when they are redeemable at the election of the holder. Rev. Ruls. 68-601, 1968-2 C.B. 124, and 89-64, 1989-1 C.B. 91.
45. Code § 409(n)(3)(B).

The Exception for Lineal Descendants of Selling Shareholders

There is an exception to the prohibited allocation rule: a total of 5% of the stock sold in the Section 1042 transaction can be allocated to a seller's lineal descendants.[46] There is no equivalent exception for lineal descendants who are considered more-than-25% shareholders by attribution. Indeed, the IRS has ruled that regardless of the 5% exception, the seller's lineal descendants are still prohibited from receiving allocations if they are more-than-25% shareholders by attribution.[47] This essentially cancels out the lineal descendant exception for many people: since the more-than-25% test is applied to the entire year before the sale, even the lineal descendants of a shareholder who owns 25% or less after the 1042 transaction will be considered more-than-25% shareholders for purposes of this test if the shareholder had more than 25% during the year before the sale. Thus, the lineal descendant exception is very narrow, applying to a seller's children only where the seller holds 25% or less of any class of stock (1) during the year preceding the sale (i.e., where the ESOP already held some stock or where the seller aggregated his or her shares with another seller's shares to reach the 30% threshold for Section 1042) *and* (2) when shares from the Section 1042 transaction are allocated within the ESOP.

Penalties for Violating the Rule

If the prohibited allocation rule is violated, the company sponsoring the ESOP must pay a 50% excise tax on the amount involved, and the person receiving the allocation is currently taxable on the value of the allocation.[48]

Procedural Requirements for the Selling Shareholder

The selling shareholder cannot simply sell to an ESOP and reinvest the proceeds in QRP without further ado. Rather, the seller must meet three procedural requirements:

---

46. Code § 409(n)(3)(A).
47. PLR 9707015 (Nov. 14, 1996).
48. Code § 7979A.

Chapter 3: Section 1042 and the Tax-Deferred ESOP "Rollover" | 67

1. The seller must elect Section 1042 treatment in a "statement of election" attached to the seller's tax return.

2. The seller must file with the statement of election a "statement of consent" from the company consenting to the imposition of excise taxes if the ESOP's three-year holding period discussed above is violated or if prohibited allocations are made.

3. The seller must file a notarized "statement of purchase" for each purchase of QRP that is made.

The IRS does not provide official forms for the statement of election, statement of purchase, or statement of consent; taxpayers and practitioners simply read the statute and regulations and follow the rather straightforward requirements set forth there.

Statement of Election

The seller must affirmatively elect Section 1042 treatment in a "statement of election" attached to the seller's income tax return for the taxable year in which the sale occurs, filed on or before the due date (including extensions of time). The 1042 election cannot be revoked once it has been made.[49] The statement of election must describe the securities sold to the ESOP, the date of the sale, the adjusted basis of the securities and the amount realized on the sale, the identity of the ESOP, and, if the sale was part of a single transaction involving other sellers, their names and taxpayer identification numbers and the number of shares they sold.[50]

Statement of Consent

The seller must file with the statement of election a verified statement of consent from the corporation consenting to the imposition of excise taxes on the corporation under Code Sections 4978 (i.e., a 10% tax if the ESOP disposes of the shares from the Section 1042

---

49. Code § 1042(a)(1), (c)(6); Temp. Treas. Reg. § 1.1042-1T, Q&A-3(a).
50. Temp. Treas. Reg. § 1.1042-1T, Q&A-3(b).

sale within three years) and 4979A (i.e., a 50% tax if a prohibited allocation is made).[51]

Statement of Purchase

For each purchase of QRP (which itself can take place only within the 15-month window of opportunity described above), the seller must execute and have notarized a "statement of purchase" declaring it to be QRP, describing it, and noting its cost and date of purchase. Originally, the IRS required the statement of purchase to be notarized within 30 days, although failure to do this on time might be excused in certain circumstances.[52] The IRS liberalized this requirement in proposed regulatory amendments issued in July 2003: the statement of purchase can be notarized any time not later than the filing of the seller's tax return for the year in which the 1042 sale occurred, or, if the QRP was purchased after that (but within the allowed period), any time not later than the filing of the seller's tax return for the year following the year in which the Section 1042 election was made.[53]

If the seller has already bought the QRP at the time of the 1042 election, the statement of purchase must be attached as part of the statement of election that is filed with the seller's tax return. Otherwise, the statement of purchase must be attached to the seller's income tax return for the year following the year in which the seller elected 1042 treatment.[54]

---

51. Code §§ 1042(b)(3), 4978(a)-(b), 4979A; Temp. Treas. Reg. § 1.1042-1T, Q&A-2(a)(4), Q&A-3(b).
52. See, e.g., PLR 200019002 (May 12, 2000) (taxpayer's delay excused where it was due to accountant's failure to inform taxpayer of this requirement).
53. REG-121122-03, Internal Revenue Bulletin 2003-37 (September 15, 2003; REG-121122-03 was originally published in the Federal Register on July 10, 2003, 68 Fed.Reg. 41087). REG-121122-03 states that taxpayers can rely on the changed rule for all open tax years pending the issuance of final regulations.
54. Temp. Treas. Reg. § 1.1042-1T, Q&A-3(b)-(c).

Consequences of Failing to Comply with the Procedural Requirements

The IRS has stated that failure to comply with procedural requirements for the Section 1042 election is not necessarily fatal where such requirements appear only in the IRS's regulations and do not go to the essence of the statute. Thus, where sellers have failed to obtain statements of purchase within 30 days of buying QRP (a purely regulatory requirement, which the IRS later moved to change as noted above), the IRS has often ruled that the sellers "substantially complied" with the regulations in those particular circumstances (for example, where the seller had immediately completed a notarized statement of purchase upon learning of the requirement for one, had filed a private letter ruling request, and/or had relied on tax professionals to prepare any necessary forms).[55]

The IRS has also applied this logic in a broader context, as when it ruled that a seller substantially complied with the requirements under Section 1042 where the seller failed to file the statement of election, statement of purchase, and statement of consent with his tax return, but then discovered these requirements and filed an amended return that incorporated these forms.[56] Please note that one is not automatically excused from complying with the Section 1042 requirements in circumstances such as the above, but rather must receive a specific ruling from the IRS pertaining to one's own situation.

---

55. See, e.g., PLR 9821022 (Feb. 17, 1998), PLR 9846015 (Aug. 13, 1998), and PLR 9852004 (Sept. 16, 1998), or PLR 200019002, noted above.
56. PLR 9619065 (May 10, 1996). However, compare *Estate of Clause v. Comm.*, 122 T.C. No. 5 (Feb. 9, 2004), in which the U.S. Tax Court held the petitioner, who sold stock to an ESOP in 1996 and purchased QRP within one year of the sale but failed to report it in any way on his tax return for 1996, could not defer recognition of tax under Section 1042 because he failed to file a timely 1042 election and thus failed to elect 1042 treatment. The petitioner in *Clause* filed amended returns (with a statement of election of Section 1042 treatment, a statement of consent from the company, and a statement of purchase of QRP) in 2001, after the IRS had commenced an audit of his 1996 return and mailed the petitioner a notice of deficiency for 1996, but to no avail.

Special Situations

There are situations in which shareholders would ordinarily not seem eligible for the Section 1042 "rollover," at least not completely, but in which proper transaction structuring can result in a complete tax deferral under Section 1042.

How to Use Seller Financing and Yet Elect Section 1042 Treatment on All the Proceeds

As discussed elsewhere in this book, sellers often finance the ESOP transaction themselves, receiving a note for the amount due. As noted above, the election to defer capital gains taxes under Section 1042 is effective only for the portion of the sale proceeds that is reinvested during the period from 3 months before to 12 months after the sale to the ESOP. This raises a problem for sellers who are financing the sale: If they have no other funds (that is, other than the proceeds from the sale to the ESOP) to invest in QRP, then some of the sale proceeds will likely be paid to them after the 15-month reinvestment period, and they will have to pay capital gains taxes on a portion of the proceeds. The fact that they are receiving the funds years after the sale does not alter this rule.[57]

There is a way out of this dilemma, however: the seller can use what is sometimes called "leveraged QRP"—that is, borrow the funds to reinvest in QRP within the 15-month reinvestment period. One method is to have the QRP serve as collateral for the loan that supplies the funds to purchase it. Investment advisors who have developed this technique use the floating-rate notes mentioned above under the heading "Qualified Replacement Property (QRP)."

How People Who Sell to *Another* Company's ESOP Can Elect Section 1042 Treatment

The most common ESOP issue in mergers and acquisitions is how the shareholder of a non-ESOP company being acquired by an ESOP company can elect the Section 1042 tax deferral for the proceeds of the

---

57. PLR 8644024 (Aug. 1, 1986).

sale.[58] There is more than one way to do it, but the transaction might be structured somewhat like this: The acquiring company already has an ESOP. The target company sets up an ESOP, which then buys the stock of the target company's shareholder, who elects Section 1042 treatment. (The acquiring company may assist in the financing or even provide financing itself.) The target company's ESOP merges into the acquiring company's ESOP, and the target company itself merges into the acquiring company. This works when either the acquirer or the target is a C corporation. While the Code does not forbid an S corporation to convert to be a C corporation to allow its shareholders to elect Section 1042 deferral and then cause the now-C corporation to merge with an S corporation, the IRS has clearly indicated it would challenge such an arrangement.

Comparative Tax Rates and the Value of Section 1042

When capital gains tax rates are historically low (as was the case after rates were reduced in 2003), Section 1042 becomes relatively less attractive, especially when the QRP might be sold at a point in the future when rates have increased. However, as of 2013, capital gains rates increased from 15% to 20% for high-income individuals and a new 3.8% Affordable Care Act Medicare surtax on the lesser of net investment income or modified adjusted gross income above $200,000 for individuals and $250,000 for married couples filing jointly[59] was added. Since gain that is excluded from income is not subject to the 3.8% surtax, this means that the Section 1042 deferral eliminates the 3.8% tax along with the capital gains tax, which in turn increases the appeal of Section 1042.

Another way in which Section 1042 became comparatively more useful in recent years is that the Tax Cuts and Jobs Act of 2017 capped the state and local tax deduction at $10,000 (including property taxes). Where a business owner in a high-tax jurisdiction once could receive millions of dollars from selling a business to an ESOP, pay hundreds of thousands of dollars in state-level taxes, and deduct those for federal

---

58. See the chapter in this book on mergers and acquisitions.
59. Code Section 1411.

purposes, that deduction is now capped at $10,000 and probably has already been used up anyway by property taxes. Thus, Section 1042 may be even more attractive to sellers after the effect of the Tax Cuts and Jobs Act of 2017, depending on which state they live in and their tax situation.

Conclusion

The tax deferral under Section 1042 helps make a leveraged sale to an ESOP the ideal business succession strategy for many shareholders of closely held companies. It allows the company to simultaneously defer or eliminate the taxation of the proceeds of the shareholder's sale of his or her shares while creating an ownership plan for the company's employees. The rules for Section 1042 are many and sometimes complex, but, as with other aspects of ESOPs, careful planning with competent legal counsel can smooth over bumps encountered on the road to employee ownership.

Chapter 4

Using ESOPs in Mergers and Acquisitions

William Merten and Vaughn Gordy

ESOPs have long provided an exit strategy for owners of privately held businesses and a platform for management buyouts. Mergers and acquisition (M&A) advisors are increasingly looking to leveraged ESOPs to accomplish both conventional stock and asset acquisitions. This chapter discusses ESOP acquisitions, together with related planning considerations, structures, corporate governance issues, and financing concerns.

General Planning Considerations

Consideration of M&A Opportunities

Considering merger and acquisition opportunities is always a challenge for a company's board of directors, but even more so if the company is partially or wholly owned by an ESOP. While some ESOP company boards do, in fact, receive company purchase offers frequently, the topic of responding to unsolicited offers is complex and certainly beyond the scope of this chapter. This chapter is focused on situations where an ESOP company's board desires to *acquire* a target company or division.

Consideration by the Board of Directors

Acquisition opportunities are usually (but not always) brought to the attention of a company's board by one or more members of its management team. In determining whether the company should offer to purchase another entity, the company's board is legally charged with a responsibility to act in the interest of all shareholders of the company. In undertaking this responsibility, board decisions are generally judged by application of the "business judgment rule," which permits a company's board members to apply their reasonable business judgment in deciding whether to pursue offers (with "business judgment" case law being developed and applied on a state-by-state basis).

Consideration by Trustee(s)

An ESOP trustee is charged with acting solely in the interest of plan participants and beneficiaries and for the exclusive purpose of providing retirement benefits. Given this charge, even in a company that is wholly owned by an ESOP, an ESOP trustee may have slightly different responsibilities than the company's board with regard to a company purchase offer. While a board's determination is judged by application of the above-described business judgment rule, the trustee is held to ERISA fiduciary standards.

Transaction Types

Once the decision is made to pursue an acquisition opportunity, the acquisition will generally be structured in one of three ways. As more fully described below, the acquiring company can (1) buy the stock or the assets of the division or company; (2) merge with the division or company; or (3) have the target company or division create a new ESOP, sell itself to the ESOP, and then merge the new ESOP with the acquirer's existing ESOP.

Due Diligence and Key Acquisition Terms

While important, arriving at a price that is agreeable to both parties to an acquisition is usually not the most difficult part of the transaction. Indeed, the time spent negotiating the purchase price will often pale in comparison to the time spent by the purchaser in its completion of thorough due diligence and the time spent by both parties in negotiating escrows, indemnifications, clawbacks, and ongoing executive compensation.

ESOP Trustee Oversight

If an ESOP trustee determines that an acquisition is going to be sizable (e.g., more than 10% of the acquirer's value), the trustee may request to be involved in the acquisition process. The trustee may want to participate in due diligence and may want to receive an opinion from its independent financial advisor that the acquisition is fair to the ESOP from a financial viewpoint. For larger transactions, the board may want to receive a similar opinion (as to fairness to all shareholders) from its own financial advisor. Although the trustee and the acquirer company will each be concerned with holding down acquisition costs, it is important that the trustee preserve the independence of its financial advisor. It may be appropriate for the acquirer's board to consider having its own financial advisor (i.e., one different from the trustee's advisor).

A company that is partially or wholly owned by an ESOP may have appointed inside employee(s) to serve as ESOP trustee(s). When a major acquisition is in the offing, inside trustee(s) may have conflicts of interest as to one or more aspects of the potential acquisition and thus may have trouble properly fulfilling applicable ERISA fiduciary duties. Should such conflicts arise, consideration should be given to the propriety of appointing either independent trustee(s) or having an independent or an institutional trustee serve as an independent fiduciary who will direct the inside trustee(s) with regard to the acquisition.

Cultural Fit

The acquirer's board will, of course, consider the strategic fit of the target company. It should also consider the cultural fit of the two organizations. Many studies suggest that this cultural fit is the most important contributor to the future success or failure of an acquisition.

Continuation, Termination, or Possible Merger of Existing Target Plans

In almost every M&A transaction, the acquirer will have to consider the disposition of existing (non-ESOP) retirement plans at the target company. The plans can either be (1) continued with amendments, (2) terminated, or (3) merged into the acquirer's existing plans. If they are continued with amendments, basic principles of plan participation, vesting, and retirement will continue to apply. These principles can give rise to multiple plan issues (e.g., minimum coverage, combined plan limits, or using dividends or distributions to sidestep applicable limits).

If the plans are merged, the acquirer must also review the target plans for possible plan and/or statutory violations. The acquirer does not want existing acquirer plans to become tainted with problems from the target plans.

If a target plan is instead terminated, its participants will become immediately vested and eligible for distributions. This can have the unintended effect of potentially placing considerable sums of money in the hands of financially inexperienced employees, possibly resulting in unexpected defections from the target employee workforce.

Finally, a decision must be made about participation by target employees in the acquirer's ESOP. If the acquirer desires to exclude target employees from its ESOP, the exclusion must comply with applicable coverage and/or separate-line-of-business requirements.[1] If, alternatively, the acquirer is prepared to bring target employees into its ESOP, decisions will have to be made regarding timing for participation and service to be counted for eligibility and vesting (with such decisions significantly affecting the acquirer's repurchase obligation, plan benefit levels, and compliance testing).

Valuation Concerns

A first valuation concern arises if the acquirer's use of cash to wholly or partially finance an acquisition has a significant temporary negative effect on the acquirer's cash flow or its ability, e.g., to make necessary capital expenditures. If it does, this fact by itself or taken with others (e.g., acquisition-related grants of dilutive stock-based compensation) may lower the per-share value of the acquirer's stock. Should this occur, the acquirer may decide to amend the plan to provide that the company will make price protection payments for certain ESOP participants whose employment may be terminated before the debt can be repaid. If it does, it will also have to determine (1) the length of the protection (e.g., whether it will last for a set period of years or until the acquisition indebtedness is repaid in its entirety), (2) the members of the

---

1. With regard to compliance testing, first see Section 410(b)(6)(c) of the Internal Revenue Code. As to separate lines of business, first see Treas. Reg. § 1.414(r)-5(d) for the safe harbor for separate lines of business acquired through certain mergers and acquisitions.

protected class (e.g., whether the class will include employees who are terminated due to death, disability, and/or normal retirement), and (3) the terms of the provided protection (e.g., whether the per-share value for the protected class will be determined (a) pursuant to a structured formula, such as one that references the new acquisition indebtedness without actually being tied to it, or (b) without regard to the entirety of the new acquisition indebtedness, but only to the extent necessary to make the post-transaction per-share value at least equal to the per-share transaction price).[2]

As a second valuation concern, it may be appropriate for each company to protect its shareholders by having its own financial advisor. Moreover, if (as described below) the transaction is structured so that an ESOP will exist at each company (even if momentarily), separate trustees and a financial advisor for each ESOP trustee will be *legally required*.[3] While multiple financial advisors can add to a transaction's cost, they may be required depending on the structure and, even if not required, having them may provide the parties (e.g., each company's board of directors) with a requisite degree of comfort.

Use of Retirement Plan and Certain IRA Assets as Transaction Consideration

It is possible, with proper safeguards and adequate disclosure, to use money transferred to the ESOP from a qualified retirement plan (including qualified plan-based IRA dollars transferred into and then from a qualified plan) as consideration in an ESOP acquisition (with any monies rolling into the ESOP from these sources being viewed by senior lender(s) as transaction equity). To the extent that non-*employer* monies will be rolled over to aid in transaction financing, it must be

---

2. On a related note, in General Legal Advice Memo 2019-3, the IRS stated that price protection payments made by the sponsoring company directly to the employee are immediately taxable (whereas such payments are not immediately taxable if the company makes a special "qualified elective contribution" to the plan that is allocated to the employee's account and then distributed as part of the eventual distribution of the account).
3. See below under "When Section 1042 Treatment is Desired by Target Shareholders: Structure."

decided how long the rollover opportunity will be extended to plan participants. Federal and state securities laws will also need to be examined for the level of required participant disclosure. Assuming that the amount of *employee* dollars being rolled over comes within federal and state securities law exemption perimeters, a registration statement will not be required. However, even if a registration statement *is not required*, at a minimum an information statement must be prepared to address applicable fraud concerns. Note that while the use of target plan (and/or IRA) monies for transaction financing can often add to the cost and complexity of a transaction, this use does serve to reduce otherwise-required transaction leverage while at the same time providing both an immediate allocation of shares and an immediate company stake to participants directing rollovers.

Use of What Had Been Matching Contributions to Repay Acquisition Indebtedness

Another general consideration when using ESOPs in mergers and acquisitions is whether the company will use what *had been* matching contributions to its 401(k) plan to repay ESOP acquisition indebtedness. Some companies will leave unchanged prior 401(k) cash matching provisions and others will not. Continuing 401(k) matching contributions while making ESOP contributions that are required to service an ESOP loan may result in unintended (and, perhaps, above-market and/or greater-than-base compensation) employee benefit levels. To the extent that such a result does not occur and/or a decision is made to still use what had been cash matching contributions to repay ESOP acquisition indebtedness, a match corresponding to 401(k) salary reduction contributions can, if desired, still be made—and it can be made without additional dollars. A provision can be drafted in the ESOP plan to provide that, instead of allocating suspense account shares under the ESOP in one step (i.e., generally pro-rata based on compensation), suspense account shares will be allocated in a two-step process. First, subject to discrimination testing, an amount of the suspense account shares to be released for the year will be allocated to ESOP participants so as to provide them with a desired benefit level corresponding to a specified percentage of the salary-reduction contributions made under the company's 401(k) plan. The remaining suspense account shares released for the year can then be allocated under the ESOP in a second step—generally, pro-rata based on compensation.

When Section 1042 Treatment Is Desired by Target Shareholders

Advantages

Once a company has adopted a leveraged ESOP, using an ESOP structure to acquire a target company can have significant advantages. First, to the extent that a target shareholder is able to sell his or her company shares to an ESOP and make a Section 1042[4] tax-deferred/tax-free election, the shareholder may be willing to pass on part of his or her income tax savings in the form of a reduced purchase price.

Second, to the extent that IRA and 401(k) dollars are rolled into the ESOP by target company employees, the amount of "outside funds" needed to acquire the target is reduced.

A third advantage is that the notion of providing seller financing will likely be much more attractive to a shareholder selling to an ESOP than it might be in a non-ESOP context. The transaction can be designed so that the seller receives (1) a note from a company to which the seller still exerts a substantial degree of post-transaction control or (2) an ESOP note that is guaranteed by such a company. The transaction can also be designed to permit the seller to obtain a higher subordinated rate of return from a company as to which the seller is inherently familiar. Moreover, assuming that the seller makes a Section 1042 election, the seller can receive cash consideration from the ESOP and then loan any desired amount of seller financing back to the company for the company's use in immediately repaying a like amount of outside (e.g., bank) debt. Such a strategy not only will permit the seller to receive a note from the company rather than the ESOP; it also will provide the seller with a basis in the note equal to the note's face so that the note's *principal* can be received by the seller tax-free. In addition, as is true in almost all ESOP purchase transactions, the transaction's timing can be easily controlled, and the transaction's occurrence can remain totally confidential (e.g., from the target's customers) until the closing of the transaction.

---

4. All section references in this chapter are to the Internal Revenue Code.

From the *acquirer's* viewpoint, in a C corporation context, both the interest and principal on the related acquisition indebtedness will be effectively tax-deductible. In an S corporation context, it may be possible to acquire a target as a subsidiary of the acquirer and then make a QSUB election so that the target's income will flow up to the acquirer (with the acquirer's income being exempt from federal, and in many cases, state, income tax to the extent it is owned by an ESOP).

Disadvantages

The principal *disadvantage* of using an ESOP to acquire another company is that the transaction structure (as described immediately below) is generally more complicated and may be more costly than a typical asset or stock acquisition structure. A second disadvantage is that the per-share price of the acquirer's ESOP stock value may decrease after the transaction for two reasons. First, as described above, the use of the acquirer's existing cash in the acquisition, either by itself or when coupled with other factors (e.g., grants of stock-based compensation), may possibly lower the per-share value of the company's shares on a post-transaction basis. Second, to the extent that the transaction is structured using the two-step ESOP-merger structure described below, the *per-share* value of the acquirer's stock may decrease due to the increase in the number of outstanding shares following the merger of the two ESOP plans.[5]

Structure

If the acquirer is a C corporation, some practitioners believe that the owner of the target shares can simply exchange his or her shares for shares of the acquirer and then sell received acquirer shares to the acquirer's ESOP (with the former target shareholder thereafter making a Section 1042 election). Because the exchange of shares will be designed to constitute a tax-free reorganization, transaction advisors will have to determine that the tax-free nature of the exchange will not be undermined by an immediate sale of the received shares to the

---

5.. Whether the increase in the number of outstanding shares will cause the per-share value of the acquirer to so drop will depend in great part on whether the target is acquired at a stock exchange rate that reflects the drop in the target's value resulting from the debt.

acquirer's ESOP. This will depend in large part on whether the advisors can determine that required reorganization "continuity" is not "busted" by the subsequent sale to the ESOP (with some practitioners believing that continuity still remains since shares are not being sold to the acquirer or a corporation related to the acquirer).[6]

If the acquirer is an S corporation (or a C corporation with advisors who believe that continuity will be broken by a post-exchange sale to an ESOP), the transaction will likely be structured so that an ESOP that is substantially identical to the acquirer's ESOP is adopted by the target to purchase shares of target shareholder(s). Once target shareholders sell their shares to the target ESOP, with the target ESOP usually using one or more ESOP note(s) for its consideration, the target will generally be merged into the acquirer or an acquirer subsidiary, with the ESOP note(s) received by the target shareholder(s) often being "cashed out" in the merger.[7] The target's ESOP will then be merged into the acquirer's ESOP (with the acquirer assuming the debt obligations of the target ESOP).

Repayment of the acquisition indebtedness will generally occur via the company's cash flow, together with:

1. dollars the target might have annually contributed as a match to its 401(k) plan, with the acquirer, again, having the ability (if desired) to continue under the ESOP any prior 401(k) "match" made by the target and/or the acquirer (with the match, again, being made within the ESOP in the form of company shares), and/or

2. dollars saved due to or because of either (a) ESOP-generated income tax deductions (in a C corporation context) or (b) the ESOP's ownership percentage that goes untaxed in an S corporation.

Administrative and Other Considerations

To the extent that the target is a C corporation that will merge into an S corporation acquirer (or an acquirer QSUB), target stock classes

---

6. In this regard, see the continuity of interest regulations at Treas. Reg. §1.368-1(e). See also PLRs 20100528 and 200052023.
7. Note that the cashing out of the ESOP note(s) so received is not an essential step; should the acquirer want to, it can pay the note(s) over time (e.g., through the ESOP), if that is the deal.

other than common will have to be converted into common before or as a part of the merger. Similarly, any target share class that has voting rights different than those in the S corporation acquirer will have to be converted before or as a part of the merger (because an S corporation can hold only voting and non-voting common shares).

To the extent that the acquirer is a C (rather than an S) corporation, an existing multi-class stock structure within either the acquirer or the target may have to be considered when merging the target into the acquirer. In addition, because C corporation ESOP loans generally are shorter than their S corporation counterparts (so as to generate larger deductions that are unnecessary in a 100% S corporation ESOP structure), tracking on a loan-by-loan basis will be required for both the dividend deduction rule of Section 404(k) and the distribution delay rule under Section 409(1)(B), which allows non-death and non-disability distributions to be delayed until the ESOP loan is repaid.

Finally, the share exchange ratio that is applicable in the merger will be the subject of much debate between the respective ESOP trustees and their advisors. For purposes of the exchange, the target may be given quite a low post-ESOP purchase value due to target company obligations on the ESOP note(s) given to the target shareholders. If this is the case, from a financial fairness viewpoint, the target financial advisors may balk at the small number of acquirer shares slated for receipt by target ESOP participants in the merger. If the target is given an equal or *higher* post-ESOP purchase value (with target participants thus slated to receive a *higher* number of shares in the merger), the acquirer will have essentially paid twice for the target: first, by cashing out the target shareholder ESOP note(s) (as a part of the merger), and second, by delivering a not-insignificant amount of acquirer shares in the merger (thereby diluting existing acquirer ESOP participants).

When Section 1042 Treatment Is Not Desired by Target Shareholders

Stock Purchase

Structure

If the acquirer is an S corporation owned wholly by an ESOP, it will not be concerned with deductions. In that case, the target seller can simply sell his or her shares to the acquirer or an acquirer subsidiary. If, on the other hand, the acquirer is a C corporation owned wholly or partially by an ESOP, deductions will be important. In that case, the transaction may be structured so that target shareholders sell their shares to an ESOP, even if they are not interested in making Section 1042 elections (so that the acquirer-controlled group will have maximized the deductions available to it). Depending upon the view of transaction advisors as to continuity (as discussed above), the target shareholders will either exchange their shares for shares of the acquirer and sell to the acquirer's ESOP, or sell their shares to a newly adopted target ESOP (with the target thereafter merging into the acquirer and the target ESOP thereafter merging into the acquirer's ESOP).

Advantages

If the target shareholder sells shares directly to the acquirer rather than to an ESOP, the advantage will be that Section 404 and Section 415 limits will never become an issue in terms of paying back the acquisition indebtedness. If a target shareholder instead sells shares to an ESOP, all of the normal ESOP advantages will be available. The seller will be able to sell stock rather than assets, which may be preferable in terms of distancing the seller from existing target liabilities. The seller also will receive cash and/or notes rather than shares of another company (as might occur in a typical merger structure). Because the seller will sell shares (rather than assets), the seller also will have a single level of taxation. In addition, because the shares are being sold to an ESOP, the seller will attain capital gains treatment on *all* of his or her sales proceeds, engage (if desired) in a totally confidential transaction, have ESOP-related advantageous seller financing (other than the tax-free receipt of principal) and *not* be asked to take a "haircut" on the price (as he or she might be asked if shares were being sold to the ESOP in a Section 1042 transaction).

From the acquisition company's viewpoint, if the target seller simply sells his or her shares to the acquisition company, both the seller and the acquirer will experience a less complex transaction, and the acquirer will not have to deal with Section 404 and 415 combined plan limits on a post-transaction basis. If, on the other hand, a target shareholder sells to an ESOP (but without making a Section 1042 election), the transaction structure will allow for the use of ESOP rollovers to reduce the amount of transaction-required financing, the use of what had previously been 401(k) matching payments to repay transaction financing, and the deductibility of both interest *and* principal. The extent to which there is a concern with maximizing the acquirer group's deductions will likely turn on whether the acquirer is operating under an S corporation election.

Disadvantages

The principal disadvantage of a target shareholder selling shares but not making a Section 1042 election is that, from the acquirer's viewpoint, the seller has no incentive to take a haircut on his or her sale price. Similarly, seller financing will not be as attractive to the seller, because—without the seller making a Section 1042 election—the transaction cannot be structured so that the seller receives seller-financing principal payments tax-free. To the extent that the target seller instead sells shares directly to the acquirer (rather than to an ESOP), principal payments on the acquisition indebtedness will not be effectively deductible. Moreover, if the acquirer is an S corporation, the seller will have assurance that *all* of his or her gain will be characterized as a capital gain (as would be the case if he or she were to sell shares to an ESOP) *only if* the seller refuses to make a Section 338(h)(10) (asset sale treatment) election.

Administrative (and Other) Considerations

If the target shareholder sells to an ESOP but *does not* make an election under Section 1042, the administrative (and other) considerations described above under "When Section 1042 Treatment Is Desired by Target Shareholders" will apply.

Asset Purchase

Structure

There may be instances in which, for liability, tax, and/or other reasons, the acquirer may want assets purchased rather than stock. Normally, the acquirer would simply purchase assets for itself (i.e., *outside* the context of its ESOP). If, however, all of the acquirer's shares were owned by an

ESOP and the acquirer wanted to flow the acquisition indebtedness through the ESOP, an asset purchase structure might be designed in a very limited circumstance to have the acquirer sell treasury shares to the acquirer's ESOP and then use received sale proceeds to purchase all or a portion of the target's ESOP.[8] If the acquirer's ESOP *does not* own 100% of the acquirer's stock, such a structure would likely not be employed since its use would dilute any existing non-ESOP shareholder. In such a case, the target's assets would be sold directly to the acquirer.

Advantages

The principal advantage of an asset sale to the seller is that the seller may be able to get a higher purchase price if the acquirer is a tax-paying C corporation. The reason is that the acquirer will be able to depreciate the purchased assets from their transaction date fair market value (thereby increasing the acquirer's deductions). If all of the acquirer's shares are owned by an ESOP, the acquirer's deductions can be even further increased in such a case if its ability to depreciate the purchased assets at their closing date fair market value is financed by the acquirer's use of treasury share sale proceeds (with the ESOP loan undertaken to permit the ESOP's purchase of treasury shares effectively allowing the acquirer to deduct acquisition indebtedness principal payments).[9]

Of course, to the extent that the acquirer is an S corporation that is wholly owned by an ESOP, deductions will be important to the acquirer group only to the extent they can be taken on applicable state tax returns. In such a case, the principal advantage of an asset purchase structure is that the acquirer may feel that it is acquiring fewer liabilities than it would were it purchasing the target's stock. (Whether this

---

8. This might occur, for example, if (1) the acquirer was a C corporation that wasn't about to become an S corporation, (2) the acquirer was in need of deductions, (3) it had no outside synthetic equity holders, and (4) it was concerned about moving more ESOP allocations to its newer employees (e.g., in a "have and have nots" scenario).

9. Such additional deductions may not be important if the acquirer can make an election to be taxed as an S corporation. There may, however, be considerations (e.g., desired retention of multiple classes of stock) which make an S corporation election impractical. In addition, even if an S corporation election will be made by a 100% ESOP-owned acquirer, state tax law considerations may make additional deductions desirable.

would actually be true would depend on the parties' relative bargaining powers in terms of purchase agreement representation and warranty and indemnification provisions.)

Disadvantages

Again, to the extent that either the acquirer's ESOP does not own 100% of the acquirer's stock or synthetic equity exists outside the ESOP, a structure involving an ESOP's purchase of acquirer treasury shares would be disadvantageous in terms of dilution to non-ESOP acquirer shareholders. From the *seller's* viewpoint, to the extent that assets rather than shares are sold, the seller will have two levels of taxation unless the target has been an S corporation for greater than a fixed number of years[10] (with the first level of taxation being incurred when the target sells the assets and the second level being incurred when the target is liquidated to the seller). A sale of the target's assets rather than its stock will mean that the target's contracts will have to be novated, which may not be required if target shares (rather than target assets) are sold.

Administrative (and Other) Considerations

The administrative and other concerns will be similar to those described above under "When Section 1042 Treatment Is Desired by Target Shareholders," including the possibility of having to track loans and/or dividends.

Acquisition Fiduciary and Settlor Issues

In every acquisition involving one or more ESOPs, normal ESOP acquisition-related fiduciary and settlor issues will arise. The transaction fiduciary will want to assure itself that the company's board is doing its job, and it may be concerned about the possible applicability of a "protected (floor) price" for ESOP shares received by participants prior to the date that new transaction indebtedness is repaid (as discussed above under "Valuation Concerns"). Examples of settlor issues that may arise include (1) an analysis as to whether the target's plans

---

10. The period was five years in 2011 and returned to ten years as of 2012.

should be amended, terminated, or merged into the acquirer's plans (as discussed above under "Continuation, Termination, or Possible Merger of Existing Target Plans"), and (2) decisions as to whether and when target employees will be brought into the acquirer's ESOP (also discussed above under "Continuation, Termination, or Possible Merger of Existing Target Plans").

Acquisition Corporate Governance Issues

Corporate governance issues that arise in acquisitions include the role of the board versus the role of plan fiduciaries and the participant voting process[11] (taking into account concerns regarding possible required pass-through votes and/or rules with regard to shareholder consents).

Both the U.S. Department of Labor and the plaintiffs' bar have become very active in reviewing ESOP transactions and litigating aggressively. In the past, there was guidance suggesting that both board of director and ESOP fiduciary meeting minutes should reflect only what was accomplished at the meeting (e.g., a vote) and not the considerations that were vetted before the resulting action(s) occurred. In the current ESOP litigation environment, this guidance has changed dramatically. In documenting an ESOP transaction, it is critically important that both board and trustee minutes reflect the discussion of the various benefits, drawbacks, and considerations that were part of any decision to proceed with the subject ESOP transaction. These minutes should reflect careful consideration and discussion of all valuation, financing, and fairness issues.

Acquisition Financing Concerns

Acquisition financing concerns include the added tax advantages of the ESOP term loan and ESOP-related seller financing, which will not be present if conventional financing is used to finance the acquisition of a

---

11. There will be a need for a participant vote at the target level if the target has an ESOP and the target will either be merging with the acquirer or selling substantially all of its assets. There will also be a need for a voting pass-through at the acquirer level in the case of a merger unless the merger is designed as a triangular merger (i.e., a merger with a subsidiary of the acquirer rather than the acquirer itself).

target. Where an ESOP purchase is included in the acquisition structure, financing-related issues will include (1) a determination of how long the term a new ESOP acquisition indebtedness should be (in terms of its impact on an existing ESOP benefit level; desired deductions, if any; and applicable contribution, dividend, and deduction limitations), (2) the impact of the acquisition on existing ESOP repurchase obligations, (3) whether participants should be given an opportunity to roll dollars into the ESOP so as to "whittle down" the required amount of ESOP acquisition indebtedness, and (4) whether matching dollars that had previously been contributed to a 401(k) plan should be used to repay ESOP indebtedness (with the match moving inside the ESOP as described above under "Use of What Had Been Matching Contributions to Repay Acquisition Indebtedness").

Conclusion

The use of an ESOP purchase structure may be advantageous in that a seller who is able to make a Section 1042 election may be willing to pass part of the seller's tax savings on to the acquirer in the form of a reduced purchase price. However, even if a Section 1042 election is *not* made by the seller, an ESOP purchase structure can permit the acquirer to purchase shares with pretax dollars, and it can allow for accessing other qualified plan and IRA monies to reduce the acquisition indebtedness. Monies that would otherwise be contributed as a 401(k) match can also be used under an ESOP purchase structure to provide a partial funding source for periodic loan payments. The factors that make seller financing so attractive under an ESOP purchase structure can also provide the structure with a competitive edge. Coupling these advantages with the manner in which ESOP financing enhances cash flow (which can be used for both debt reduction and periodic growth) may, in fact, make the ESOP structure a worthy alternative to traditional M&A acquisition structures in many situations. An ESOP purchase structure can also serve as a go-forward investment and/or acquisition platform. Finally, the use of an ESOP as a stalking horse and/or acquisition tool may also provide an acquirer or an M&A firm with advantage(s) not found elsewhere.

With proper planning, the considerations that have to be explored and quantified in any ESOP structure need not become structural drawbacks. In an economy in which M&A advisors and private equity groups are looking for flexible structures they can use to take an acquisition to completion, the leveraged ESOP purchase structure presents a compelling alternative. Although beyond the scope of this chapter, the structure's use may also make an ESOP an appropriate acquisition vehicle in the case of a desired divestiture (including a spinoff of a division or company, e.g., a failed "roll-up" company) and/or a private equity group that is seeking to liquidate its equity investment in a "sideways" company.

Chapter 5

Bank and Seller Financing for ESOP Transactions

David Solomon and Regina Carls

The large majority of ESOP transactions are financed either by loans from banks or a combination of bank loans and subordinated promissory notes issued to the sellers in exchange for shares. In some cases, other forms of capital that are in a junior position to senior bank debt are raised to provide additional cash proceeds to the sellers. These forms of capital may include second-lien debt, mezzanine debt (unsecured debt subordinated to the bank debt) or structured equity (unsecured debt subordinated to senior and mezzanine debt). These forms of capital are discussed in detail in chapter 7. Structured equity has equity warrants attached to notes. Equity warrants give the holder the right to purchase a certain number of newly issued shares of stock for a price set in the contract. This price is usually the post-transaction value determined after giving effect to the ESOP transaction. This allows the holder to realize an incremental return from the capital appreciation of the stock. According to NCEO data, about 20% of seller notes also include equity warrants. Chapter 6 discusses warrants. This chapter focuses only on bank loans and seller notes.

How ESOP Financing Works

Chapter 1 discussed the basic structure of an ESOP loan. In most cases, the ESOP loan is funded by the company with the proceeds of a loan from a bank. The steps involved in an ESOP loan are as follows:

- Step 1: The lender loans money to the company sponsoring the ESOP, which is referred to as the "outside" loan. Usually the funds representing the "outside" loan come from a loan from a bank to the company.
- Step 2: The company then lends the funds represented by the "outside" loan to the ESOP trust, which is referred to as the "inside" loan.
- Step 3: The ESOP trust uses the funds representing the "inside" loan to buy stock of the company from the seller.

Figure 5-1 illustrates the process for funding the purchase of company stock from the selling company shareholders by using the "outside" loan and the "inside" loan.

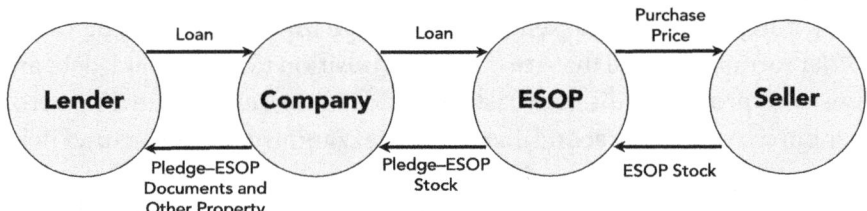

Figure 5-1. Process for funding ESOP transaction with outside and inside loans

The terms of the "outside loan" and the "inside loan" are almost never the same. The bank that makes the "outside loan" to the company will want that loan to be paid under terms that are customary to most bank loans that are used to fund buyouts, including having the loan amortize and mature between five to seven years from issuance. In addition, the company can repay the "outside loan" faster than its terms if the company is performing well. In many cases, the bank will even require the company to prepay the "outside loan" with a negotiated percentage of the company's "excess" cash flow.

Unlike the "outside loan," which is the ultimate source of capital to finance the sellers' proceeds, the key feature of the "inside loan" is to govern the pace at which participants earn their benefits in the plan. The longer the tenor (length of time until it is due) of the "inside loan," the longer the period during which the company can allocate shares to employees. This allows the company to provide a benefit from the ESOP for current as well as future employees. In addition, the payment of the "inside loan" is supported by contributions of cash by the company to the ESOP trust so that the ESOP trust will have the funds to make the necessary principal and interest payments for the "inside loan." The IRS limits the amount that a company can contribute to the ESOP trust each year to a specified percentage of the company's annual payroll (this limit is generally 25% of covered payroll). Therefore, "inside loan" debt service must fit within the legal limits on annual contributions. As a result, the term of the "inside loan" is typically at least 20 years and in many cases is much longer (up to 50 years in some cases). Figure 5-2 highlights how these loans work.

Mechanics of a Leveraged ESOP Transaction Structure

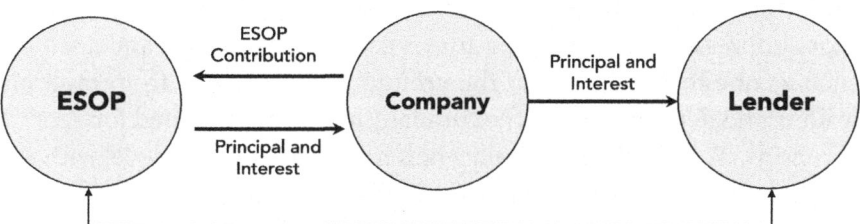

ESOP Stock Allocated to Participant Accounts

Transaction Process

1. Bank loans money to company, creating the external loan
2. Company loans money to ESOP to fund the purchase, creating the internal loan
3. ESOP uses proceeds to purchase shares from seller
4. Purchased shares are held in "suspense" as collateral for the internal loan

Employee Allocations

1. Company makes pretax contribution to ESOP trust
2. ESOP receives contribution and immediately repays the internal loan, causing a release of shares
3. Company receives funds from the ESOP and pays back the external loan
4. The resulting flow of funds provides a tax deduction to company with no impact to cash flow

Figure 5-2. Mechanics of a leveraged ESOP transaction

The Process for Obtaining Bank Financing for an ESOP Transaction

When deciding on how to obtain financing, many borrowers look first to banks. This is very often the lowest-cost approach.

The process for obtaining an ESOP loan is similar to that required for any other bank financing. However, there will be additional ESOP-specific diligence items required. As with most financings, banks will look for up to five years of outside accountant-prepared historical financial statements and the most recent interim financial statements with the corresponding prior-year period. In addition, the bank will want company-prepared projections for a minimum of five years to correspond with the term of the bank financing. The projections are important because they demonstrate how the company will tolerate leverage and how it will be able to repay its debt. Therefore, developing a well-reasoned long-term projection is a key part of the overall financing process. Banks will be more impressed with a forecast that is carefully developed and justified, such as one that builds from the ground up, with input from multiple leaders and departments in the company and is stress-tested for various scenarios. To help the bank gain a better feel and comfort level with the company, it will be very useful to explain the rationale for the factors that drive revenue growth, profit margins, capital expenditures, and other investment requirements, and how the company turns[1] its operating assets (such as accounts receivable and inventory).

Banks will require information about specific tangible assets that are looked to as loan collateral. For example, loans are often secured by accounts receivable and inventory. Banks will examine detailed accounts receivable aging reports and inventory lists, prepared on a current basis. In addition, banks will often look at summary historical information prepared on a monthly or quarterly basis to assess how these assets fluctuate to determine the level of collateral coverage they provide throughout the year. Banks often require a field exam before providing financing to determine whether there are portions of the receivable and

---

1. Asset turns is the ratio computed by dividing average yearly assets into average yearly sales. More turns are generally a good sign. Asset turns can be computed as well by focusing just on some assets, such as inventory or accounts receivable.

inventory collateral base that should be excluded or treated differently, based upon the bank's credit policies. Where reliance is placed on real estate and fixed assets, banks seek lists of properties and equipment. If specific values are placed on these assets, they will require appraisals to determine the likely realizable value if they were liquidated.

Management is a critical factor in any bank's evaluation of a loan request. The company should provide background information on its management team and make them available to the bank to meet. If a seller held an active management position in the company and is now leaving the company's employment, it is important to explain the impact to the company's operation of this person's departure, particularly as it relates to the potential impact on vital customer or vendor relationships. Banks will also want a sufficient amount of collateral for the loan. Hence, as part of the underwriting process, the bank will expect to receive a detailed accounts receivable aging report, inventory lists, fixed asset schedules, and equipment appraisals.

In addition to the above, which is standard for most financing requests, there are additional ESOP-specific requirements the bank will generally require. For S corporation ESOPs, banks will require a pro-forma 409(p) test (anti-abuse test) showing the company's 409(p) position after giving effect to the transaction. For second-stage transactions (i.e., where an existing ESOP purchases some or all of the remaining outstanding shares of its sponsor), banks will likely require a current repurchase obligation study. Repurchase obligation studies provide the bank with an estimate of the liability the company (the plan sponsor) has to buy back stock of departing ESOP participants. While this is not likely to be a requirement for evaluating a financing of a new ESOP because repurchase obligations are generally not large enough during the first 7 to 10 years after the initial ESOP transaction, banks will often require that one be performed within the first few years after the transaction and then periodically thereafter. Finally, while the bank is not entitled to receive a copy of the valuation report prepared for the trustee in support of the fairness opinion, the bank will often seek to review the fairness opinion letter to understand the scope of the analysis performed and the breadth of the opinion. Going forward, the bank may request a copy of the annual update valuations and will be prepared to sign a non-reliance letter for the trustee if requested.

When approaching a bank to help finance an ESOP transaction, the company and sellers should go in with a plan. They should know the general deal parameters—how much will be sold, the price being offered to the ESOP, the sellers' desired level of cash proceeds, and the company's overall comfort level with debt and how much it thinks it can handle. They should also make sure that the bank understands how the negotiation process around the ESOP's price works and that it can fluctuate during the process. Make sure you know what bank covenants (such as coverage ratios) are, what will trigger them, and what flexibility there is if you cannot meet a covenant in a quarter.

A company should not assume that all bankers will know how ESOPs work. Some do, and if you can find one who does, there is a considerable benefit to that. But most won't and will need education on the structure of a leveraged ESOP, the tax benefits an ESOP provides that makes loan repayment easier, how an ESOP can improve or cement a good corporate culture, the ability to use deductible dividends to repay the loan, and how to understand the accounting treatment for ESOPs.

As an example, the bank may need to be educated on the impact of the "inside loan" on the company's balance sheet. Since the economic effect of an ESOP transaction is similar to a traditional leveraged recapitalization, GAAP principles require an accounting treatment that reflects that impact. Therefore, while it may seem logical that the "inside loan" be booked as an asset of the company (after all, the ESOP's obligation is to the company), GAAP instead treats it as a contra-equity account in the shareholder equity section of the company's balance sheet. This often results in a negative net total equity, which would make the company appear to be insolvent. A company may want its accountant to help explain why this is not really an issue.

It is important to emphasize to potential lenders that ESOP companies have a strikingly good track record for successful performance when they are employee-owned. NCEO research during the 2009–2013 period (covering the period of the Great Recession) showed that among almost 1,700 ESOP loans studied in a representative sample, the default rate was two per thousand per year. A company working with its incumbent bank should also stress that doing an ESOP means the company stays independent to retain its existing financing and other relationships. Conversely, selling to a private equity firm or competitor may likely cause the bank to lose the client relationship.

Financing Terms

As with nearly all bank financings, the company will be required to satisfy certain covenants set forth by the bank. The covenants required and the testing frequency will vary based on the loan; however, it is customary to see either a debt service coverage test (DSC) or a fixed charge coverage test (FCC) as well as a maximum leverage test and/or a minimum EBITDA requirement. Depending on how leveraged the transaction is at close, there may be a requirement for an annual excess cash flow requirement to be applied to the financing, typically until leverage falls below a targeted threshold.

Similar to covenants, bank terms and loan rates are highly customized based on the loan request. Every bank has its own profitability model that is run for each loan request. Companies should appreciate that there is a direct connection between credit risk and pricing. Banks have capital requirements, and capital has a cost, as it does for all companies. The higher the overall riskiness of a bank's portfolio, the greater its capital requirements and the greater its capital costs. Therefore, the bank will use the risk grade that it concludes from its credit analysis as a discrete input into its pricing analysis. Pricing is typically based on LIBOR, and the spread above LIBOR will be determined based on the riskiness of the loan.[2] While loan terms are also highly customized, as previously noted it is customary to see a five-year tenor for most ESOP financings, with amortization schedules varying between five and seven years depending on the situation.

As stated previously, not every bank has a dedicated ESOP team in place and therefore may not have a detailed understanding of how an ESOP affects the financials of the sponsoring company. The financial impacts vary based on the structure of the ESOP financing, whether it is a C or S corporation, and what other forms of capital (beyond senior debt) are deployed to finance the transaction. It is essential to understand all of these factors will affect the loan not only at inception but

---

2. Note that LIBOR will be phased out in 2021 and replaced with another standard measure.

also throughout the life of the loan. As a result, it is important to select a bank that has a detailed knowledge of these issues and can structure the loan and covenant package accordingly. The relevant associations have a listing of the various financing sources active in the ESOP space as well as other practitioners active in the space who can provide recommendations. It is always good to solicit a few banks to compare and contrast the various terms and conditions each bank provides. This allows the company to see how banks and financing sources vary and also provides the company with a competitive market deal.

Seller Financing for ESOP Transactions

In many ESOP transactions, a company cannot borrow enough in senior debt to finance the entire ESOP transaction. In some cases, a company may be unable to borrow, or prefers not to borrow, any funds on a senior basis to fund the purchase price. In these cases, financing from the sellers is typically used to finance the gap. Where seller notes are used, the objective is to have the company ultimately be the issuer of the note to the sellers. This allows the sellers to have a creditor's claim on the company's assets (subject to priority liens generally provided in favor of more senior lenders). When sellers hold notes issued by the ESOP, they can be secured only by the unallocated shares held by the ESOP that were purchased with the financing the seller provided. There are significant restrictions embedded in the seller notes around declaring a default and accelerating repayment that would not exist in the seller notes. Perhaps more importantly, seller notes issued by the ESOP can only be repaid through a contribution to the ESOP and a subsequent debt payment. This process will allocate shares, thus restricting a company's willingness or ability to prepay the seller debt. In many cases, the ESOP will issue the notes to the seller at the close of the transaction, quickly followed by a "day loan" set of transactions that within days shifts the seller note issuance to the company in exchange for a replacement note between the company and the ESOP.

Like the bank debt, the seller notes will charge interest on the face value of the note. Seller notes are junior to any other kind of debt and therefore could conceptually command an interest rate at least comparable to third-party mezzanine debt rates (typically in a range of 12%–15%). However, seller notes are very often priced well below those levels to allow the company to tolerate the higher debt levels and thereby facilitate the transaction. NCEO data indicates that sellers who receive notes in exchange for their stock in an ESOP transaction usually settle for rates more in the 6% to 9% range. As previously noted, in approximately 20% of ESOP transactions, sellers receive warrants that are attached to their notes, allowing them to earn a return through the appreciation of the company's stock. This provides the sellers with an incremental source of return on their note, pushing total rates of return above 10%. This may also allow a seller to take an even lower rate of cash-pay interest to further improve the company's overall cash flow dynamics after the transaction closes.

Deals that include warrants as part of the seller financing have been a target of some Department of Labor (DOL) investigations. In these investigations, the DOL has asserted that the company issued too many warrants or their payment terms were too aggressive, so it is critical to make sure the terms of the warrants are fair and reflect a market rate of return for the risk the seller is taking by financing the ESOP's purchase of stock.

Seller notes can also be structured so that the interest and principal of the seller note is not paid year to year but rather fully or partially deferred to the end of the term. The accumulated interest may also be added to the principal amount of the seller note ("payment-in-kind" [PIK] interest) and also accrue interest subject to an interest rate and paid at the end of the term of the seller note. The deferred payment of principal and interest on the seller notes and PIK interest create several tax considerations for the seller, which should be carefully reviewed with a tax advisor to fully understand the tax consequences.

Choosing Between Bank Financing and Seller Notes

There are various reasons why people considering an ESOP transaction will choose to obtain bank financing or use seller notes.

One reason to use bank financing is that having a loan from a bank to fund all or a portion of the ESOP's purchase of stock is that it makes it easier for the seller to take advantage of the Section 1042 rollover treatment, which is described in more detail in chapter 3. In a 1042 transaction, sellers have the ability to defer capital gains treatment on the sale of stock to an ESOP in a C corporation if the ESOP ends up with 30% or more of the shares. They have three months before the sale and 12 months after to make the investment in "qualified replacement property." However, the seller needs cash from the sale of their shares of stock to the ESOP trust to be able to invest in qualified replacement property.

If the ESOP transaction is funded in whole or in part with a bank loan, then the company can make the "inside loan" to the ESOP trust, which will then have the cash necessary to buy the seller's stock so that the seller can then use that cash to purchase the qualified replacement property. However, if there is no bank financing and instead there are only seller notes issued and they are to be repaid in installments, the seller cannot simply invest each installment in the qualified replacement property. They still only have 12 months to meet the requirements to re-invest the proceeds from the sale in qualified replacement property. While there are workarounds to this issue when an ESOP transaction is funded with seller notes, as explained in chapter 3, these workarounds involve more transaction costs and complexity, at least for some period of time, which makes bank financing more compelling in Section 1042 transactions.

Even when sellers do not elect to defer capital gains taxes, obtaining bank financing is still attractive because it provides the sellers with some cash at closing to cover capital gain taxes and to use for other purposes.

As noted earlier, banks have a limit on how much they will loan—no bank will finance a 100% ESOP unless there is an unusual amount of collateral (how much banks will loan is discussed below). Seller notes are then commonly used to fill the gap. Many sellers, however, prefer not to get banks involved at all and do all the financing through notes. They may do this to avoid the extra time and expense of obtaining a bank loan, because they find the interest rate they can get on the notes appealing, and/or they want the flexibility of a seller note if the company doesn't perform as planned and would struggle meeting the loan covenants on bank financing.

The amount of each type of financing for ESOP transactions are based on market multiples of EBITDA or similar measures. Table 5-1 shows the key measures involved for determining how much of each type of financing is available and the costs.

Table 5-1. ESOP financing transaction metrics

Type of financing	Expected return	EBITDA turn*/amount
Senior (bank) debt	4%–6%	2–3x EBITDA
Mezzanine lender	12%–15%	1–1.5x EBITDA
Seller notes/warrants	10%–13%	Balance of purchase price

*An EBITDA turn is the ratio of the debt to one year's EBITDA.

Table 5-2 presents an additional way to compare whether to obtain bank versus seller financing.

Table 5-2. Financing: bank vs. seller

	Bank	Seller
Proceeds at closing	✓	
Diversification	✓	
Control/flexibility		✓
Oversight	✓	
Upside opportunity		✓
Interest income		✓
Quick close		✓

As mentioned above, if a seller needs cash up front for investing in "qualified replacement property" for a Section 1042 election, they will typically want and need some bank financing. However, a company that does not want to have a bank involved in its capital structure or that is not equipped to manage the reporting and compliance requirements of a bank loan will lean more toward seller financing. If a deal needs to close on a tight time frame (e.g., to close before the end of the tax year to lock in tax benefits or due to ill health of the seller), then seller financing may be the way to go instead of going through the complex process to get bank financing in place. All of these factors need to be considered before choosing whether to obtain bank financing, solely use seller financing, or use a combination of the two options (along with mezzanine debt, which chapter 7 covers). This does not have to be a "one and done" decision. Many ESOP companies that used seller financing reach back out to a bank in three to five years after the initial sale transaction to refinance some or all of the seller notes issued at the time of the sale of the stock to the ESOP as a way to finally cash out the seller and/or to lower the company's cost of capital.

Chapter 6

Warrants in ESOP Transactions

Philip J. Carstens

As discussed in chapter 5, warrants are used in about 20% of all ESOP financing, almost always in conjunction with a seller note. The seller agrees to take a lower interest rate in return for some number of warrants. A warrant is a derivative security that gives the holder the right to purchase securities, normally common stock of the corporation issuing the warrant ("issuer"), at a specific price (the "strike price" or "exercise price") on a particular date or within a predetermined timeframe (the "exercise window").

In ESOP transactions, warrants are often coupled with promissory notes to the seller to create "investment units," a way to provide the seller with an interest rate on the note plus a chance to gain some of the future upside performance of the company. While most often created at the time of the initial transaction, sometimes a seller may agree at some later point to a lower rate of interest or forgiveness on part of the note due in return for some number of warrants.

Warrants issued in ESOP transactions are a financing tool used to provide sellers with an overall targeted internal rate of return (IRR). A warrant is best understood as a strategy for increasing the targeted yield for sellers who receive subordinated notes with low coupon interest rates in an ESOP transaction.

Warrants should not be viewed as an addition to the purchase price, but rather as a way to give sellers a market return for the risk associated with holding riskier debt. If the ESOP transaction is done partly with bank financing, the seller note is subordinated; if the entire transaction is via a seller note, the seller's only collateral is the stock of the company the seller already owns. So either way, a seller note is riskier debt than a secured senior loan and thus normally should get a higher rate of return.

How Warrants Are Structured

When setting up a warrant structure, it is essential to get advice from qualified professionals. The transaction needs to be designed by an ESOP attorney, subject to a fairness opinion from an outside appraisal firm, and reviewed by the ESOP trustee to make sure the terms are fair to the plan participants.

Warrant certificates often include put and call rights. A put right gives the warrant holder the right to put the warrant to the issuer (cause the issuer to purchase the warrant from the warrant holder) at or before the expiration of the exercise window.

A call right gives the issuer the right to call the warrant (cause the warrant holder to sell the warrant to the issuer) at or before the expiration of the exercise window. The issuer normally will want the right to call the warrant even if the holder has exercised the purchase right contained in the warrant so that the warrant can be settled in cash rather than in shares of stock. This is certainly the case for ESOP owner S corporation issuers in order to preserve the corporation's S status and 100% ESOP ownership status.

It has been suggested that a warrant could be designed with no exercise purchase right. If an option (warrant) doesn't contain an option to purchase, is it really an option? Probably not. If it is not an option, the taxation implications are not clear.

Warrants created in connection with ESOP transactions should include provisions protecting the ESOP in the event of unanticipated occurrences. Such occurrences include major corporate transactions such as a sale, merger, recapitalization, or termination of the ESOP.

For example, an unanticipated sale of the company at a premium price shortly after an ESOP transaction raises equity allocation issues. Absent event protection language in the transaction documents, the warrant holder may be allocated a disproportionate amount of the transaction premium to the disadvantage of the ESOP. The warrant certificate and/or the purchase agreement should address these issues. A trustee may refuse to do the deal without a limitation on the amount of the allocation of the sale premium to the warrant holder.

The warrant should provide that the number of warrants will be adjusted in the event of the sale of cheap stock, issuance of a stock dividend, contribution of stock to the ESOP, or stock splits. Likewise, the number of warrants should be adjusted to reflect a reduction in the number of the issuer's issued and outstanding shares due to a redemption. Such an adjustment is necessary to protect the ESOP's claim on equity. In either case, the holder's or the ESOP's claim on equity should remain constant.

Corporate Tax Issues

Many investment unit strategies are structured to enable the issuer to maintain its S corporation status or elect S corporation status following the ESOP transaction. S corporations can only have one class of stock.[1]

Investment units can look a lot like stock. If the investment units were ultimately determined to be a second class of stock, the tax outcome would be disastrous. For this reason, investment units in ESOP warrant deals are designed to comply with the straight debt safe harbor in Treas. Reg. 1.1361- 1(1)(5) and the option safe harbor in Treas. Reg. 1.1361-1(1)(4).

The straight debt safe harbor provides that a note will not be treated as a second class of stock if it is a written unconditional promise to pay a sum certain on demand or on a specified date, and the note:

1. Must not provide for an internal rate or payment dates that are contingent on profits, the borrower's discretion, or similar factors.

2. Must not be convertible (directly or indirectly) into stock or any other equity interest in the S corporation.

3. Must be held by an individual (other than a nonresident alien), an estate, or a trust described in Code Section 1361(c)(2).

To comply with these requirements, notes issued as part of an investment unit in an ESOP transaction are straightforward and contain restrictions limiting ownership of such notes to eligible S corporation shareholders.[2]

The warrant component of an investment unit must also be designed to comply with the option safe harbor in Treas. Reg. 1.1361-1(4)(iii)(C).

---

1. Internal Revenue Code ("Code") Section 1361(b)(1)(D).
2. Code Section 1361(b)(1)(B) and (C).

The regulations provide that the warrant, when issued, must have a strike price equal to at least 90% of the fair market value of the underlying share subject to the warrant. If the warrant is thereafter transferred to a holder who is not an eligible S corporation shareholder, the strike price must be adjusted to equal 90% of the fair market value of the underlying share on the date of transfer.

Strike Price

As indicated above, the warrant strike price must be at least 90% of the fair market value of the underlying stock that is subject to the option on the date of issuance.

The fair market value of the underlying shares may be the transaction value or post-transaction value. Either value can be used; however, the selection of the valuation date has a significant impact on how many warrants are issued—the higher the strike price, the more warrants that must be issued to achieve the targeted return. With a lower strike price, fewer warrants need to be issued to achieve the targeted return.

Analytical Framework in Determining the IRR and Number of Warrants to Be Issued

When analyzing an ESOP transaction involving the use of investment units, care should be taken to ensure that the return to the seller does not exceed a reasonable and appropriate return, given existing capital market costs for debt financing with similar risk characteristics.

- The IRR generated should be viewed in the context of the various slices of the issuer's capital structure that the investment unit is replacing.
- An investment unit in an ESOP transaction will provide sub-debt rates of return. The "blended" yield on the investment unit is the total yield of the promissory note coupon rate and the warrant yield. During 2020, blended yields for investment units have been seen in the range of 9.5% to 11.5%.
- The number of shares issuable upon exercise of the warrant issued in connection with the promissory note is referred to as "warrant

coverage." Warrant coverage and conversion discounts are mechanisms to compensate the selling shareholder for providing financing.

- Warrant coverage ultimately is negotiated between the issuer and the selling shareholders, but some of the more important elements considered in arriving at warrant coverage include (1) the estimated value of the underlying stock in the future when the warrant may be executed, (2) the strike price, (3) the estimated term the warrants will be outstanding, and (4) the estimated dilution of equity of the issuer in the future when the warrant is exercised.

The starting point for determining the number of warrants to be issued is the targeted IRR (coupon plus warrant proceeds). The issuer must determine how soon its cash flow will enable it to pay the subordinated note. If the stated term of the subordinated note is 10 years but the issuer anticipates cash flow will enable it to pay the notes in 8 years, then the 8-year term should be used in calculating the number of warrants to be issued to achieve the target IRR.

The issuer then must estimate the projected share value of the stock subject to the warrant at the most likely date on which the warrant will be settled. The parties' financial advisors must estimate the cash to be received by the seller on the repayment of the note (principal and interest):

- Face value of seller note (initial outlay), plus
- Cash received from repayment of principal and interest on the note, plus
- Cash payment on the warrants

The concluded IRR should be compared with capital market pricing for debt financing with similar risk characteristics. In my experience, warrant coverage does not generally exceed 16%–18% of equity on a fully diluted basis.

Valuation of Warrants

The parties to an ESOP transaction involving warrants may find it necessary or convenient to consider the following:

- A determination of whether the transaction creates original issue discount (OID) income under Code Section 1273(c)(2) and Treas. Reg. § 1.1273-2(h)(1) (the "investment unit rule"). If the investment unit rule applies, it will be used to determine the issue price of the subordinated note and the amount of OID generated by the investment unit.

- It may be appropriate to calculate the value of a warrant issued in the exchange note strategy described above. If the strategy results in recognized gain on the issue of the warrant, the amount of the gain will be equal to the value of the warrant.

- The issuer will be required to value warrants issued in an ESOP transaction for financial statement presentation purposes. Warrants issued in ESOP transactions will likely be settled for cash. Therefore, the warrants will be reflected as a liability on the issuer's financial statement.

- The warrants will need to be valued if they are gifted or are included in a deceased holder's estate.

An issuer or fiduciary determining the value of the warrant necessarily must rely upon value analysis performed by a qualified financial advisor. The financial advisor will select an appropriate valuation method or combination of methods. Common valuation approaches include:

- *Intrinsic value:* The intrinsic value of a warrant is the difference between the fair market value of the underlying share and the warrant strike price at the time the warrant is valued. (If the warrant is not in the money, the intrinsic value will equal zero). The calculation is complex and needs to be performed by an expert.

- *Closed-form model* (e.g., the Black-Scholes-Merton ("BSM") formula):
  — Best for public companies
  — Best for "plain-vanilla" time-based vesting awards
  — Less applicable for awards with vesting based on market conditions or that include unique factors

- *Lattice model* (e.g., a binomial model)
  — Inputs can vary based on different scenarios as time progresses
  — Best for awards with vesting based on market conditions or for issuing companies with evolving fundamentals
- *Monte Carlo simulation*
  — Flexible and allows for unique circumstances specific to the security or award being valued
  — A system that uses random numbers to measure possible outcomes and the likelihood of occurrence
  — Certain key variables change randomly based on an expected distribution
  — Results in a probability distribution of outcomes and confidence intervals (i.e., probabilities of being "correct")
  — The analysis must identify and define key uncertain assumptions (i.e., inputs) that are material to the analysis, including any anticipated correlation, and define a probability distribution
    — Pros: Probabilistic model—inputs are dynamic, approximates real world results
    — Cons: More assumptions, limited practicability, replication
  — Practical for awards with complex vesting based on market conditions

Fairness Opinions in Leveraged ESOP Transactions Involving Investment Units

As ESOP transactions have become more complicated, trustees are requesting more comprehensive financial fairness opinions from their financial advisors. The most basic fairness opinions rendered in opinion letters requested by ESOP trustees are commonly referred to opinions regarding "absolute fairness." These opinions typically give trustees comfort that the proposed transaction fits into an exemption to the prohibited transaction rules of the Employee Retirement Income Security Act of 1974 (ERISA) and the Code. The transaction components giving rise to these opinions involve actions between the ESOP and parties in interest (ERISA Section 3(14)) or disqualified persons (Code Section 4975(e)(2)). Examples of absolute fairness opinions include:

Adequate Consideration/Fairness

The prohibited transaction provisions found in ERISA Section 406 and Code Section 4975 generally prohibit transactions between a plan and a "party in interest." Without an exemption from the prohibited transaction rules, an ESOP could not acquire employer stock from the employer or from other parties in interest (such as major shareholders, officers, and directors).

An exemption from the prohibited transaction rules, pursuant to ERISA Section 408(e), permits an ESOP to acquire employer securities from any party in interest, provided that (among other requirements) the purchase price paid by the ESOP is not more than "adequate consideration."

ERISA Section 3(18) defines "adequate consideration" for purposes of this "sale" exemption to mean the fair market value of the security as determined in good faith by the fiduciary pursuant to the terms of the plan and in accordance with regulations promulgated by the U.S. Department of Labor (DOL). Code Section 401(a)(28)(C) and common practice requires an ESOP to obtain valuations by an independent appraiser of employer securities that are not readily tradeable on an established securities market.

A financial opinion that the transaction consideration does not exceed adequate consideration is an absolute fairness opinion. Such opinions should document the analysis and diligence process by the appraiser rendering the opinion.

Reasonable Interest Rate and Loan Terms

ERISA Section 406(a)(1)(B) and Code Section 4975(c)(1)(B) include as a prohibited transaction any "direct or indirect . . . lending of money or other extension of credit between a plan and a party in interest" (or disqualified person). Without an exemption, this provision would prohibit any debt financing for the acquisition of employer stock by an ESOP where a party in interest extends credit through a direct loan, a loan guarantee, or an installment sale.

ERISA Section 408(b)(3) and Code Section 4975 (d)(3) provide an exemption from the prohibited transaction rules. This exemption permits an ESOP to borrow money using a direct loan, loan guarantee, or installment sale from a party in interest to effect its acquisition of employer stock.

ERISA and the Code require that the interest rate must be reasonable. This requirement is interpreted in the regulations as meaning that the rate must not exceed a reasonable rate. The regulations provide that all relevant factors will be considered in determining a reasonable rate of interest, including:

- the amount and the duration of the loan;
- the security and guarantee (if any) involved;
- the credit standing of the ESOP and the guarantor (if any), and
- the interest rate prevailing for comparable loans.

A fairness opinion issued to an ESOP trustee by its appraiser regarding adequate consideration and the loan exemption are examples of absolute fairness opinions. Note that the common characteristic of the absolute fairness opinions is that they implicate a transaction that is subject to ERISA.

Relative Fairness

Relative fairness opinions do not implicate the prohibited transaction rules and exemptions regarding transactions between an ERISA fiduciary and an interested party or disqualified person. For example, the issuance of the investment units in the alternative structures described above does not implicate action by the ESOP; in fact, the ESOP cannot legally issue warrants.

Financial opinions regarding the issuance of investment units typically involve the relative fairness to the constituent parties including the issuer, the seller and indirectly the ESOP. Such opinions may include:

- Dilution: An opinion that the issuance of the investment units will not excessively dilute the equity interest of the ESOP.
- Yield: An opinion that the IRR flowing from the investment units does not exceed a market yield on similar instruments, given the risk of comparable debt.
- Overall fairness: An opinion that the overall transaction (price, yield terms) is fair to the ESOP from a financial point of view.

The trustee may require an opinion from its appraiser as to the relative fairness of the transaction taken as a whole. These relative fairness opinions, unlike the absolute fairness opinions discussed above, are not focused on whether the transaction fits within an exemption to the prohibited transaction rules but rather are focused on whether the trustee has fulfilled its fiduciary duty under ERISA Section 404.

Critical deal points will include the term of the subordinated note and the exercise window of the warrant. The term of the subordinated note will be analyzed and determined in the context of the company's ability to pay the note.

Examples of Warrant Strategies

C Corporation Alternative 1: 100% Sale

If the transaction involves a C corporation, the selling shareholders may desire to take advantage of deferring the recognition of the income realized as a result of the transaction by using the provisions of Code Section 1042. The benefits of Section 1042 apply only to sales of stock issued by the ESOP sponsor to an ESOP. The rules for the tax deferral require that the seller reinvest the gains in qualifying employer securities within 3 months before or 12 months after the sale. The seller cannot just take each payment on the note and reinvest it and defer the gains. If the seller does not have the funds from other sources to get the full deferral, there are investment vehicles, as described in chapter 3, to solve this problem. This chapter does not address the issues that need to be considered to qualify for Section 1042 treatment. Rather it addresses the investment unit structure that can be used in connection with Section 1042 transactions.

Assume the seller wants to sell 100% of the stock. This warrant structure involves the ESOP purchasing the stock offered in the transaction in exchange for cash and subordinated ESOP notes. The subordinated ESOP notes are then exchanged for investment units consisting of a note(s) between the company and the seller for a stated rate of interest and warrants. The exchange occurs as part of the closing of the transaction.

Immediately following the transaction, the ESOP will be the 100% owner of the issued and outstanding stock of the issuer. The tax consequences of this strategy are:

- Compliance with provisions of Section 1042 will enable the selling shareholder to defer the recognition of the gain realized on the sale.

- The Affordable Care Act (ACA) 3.8% Medicare surtax on income will not apply because Code Section 1411(C) defines net investment income as net gain (to the extent taken into account in computing taxable income) attributable to the disposition of property. If a Section 1042 election is made with respect to the shares sold, no gain will be recognized. If no gain is recognized, the realized gain will not be taken into account in computing taxable income.

- In the event the seller elects not to defer recognition under Section 1042, the gain realized will be recognized and taxed when received. Additionally, the net investment gain will be subject to tax under the provisions of Code Section 1411.

- This exchange note strategy may result in the recognition of a small amount of long-term capital gain as a result of the issuance of the warrant (Code Section 1001 (b)). The amount of the gain will be based on the value of the warrant(s) issued as a part of the transaction. Such recognition will offset gain subsequently recognized when the warrant is put or called. (However, any gain recognized as a result of the exchange will not be subject to the Code Section 1411 tax on net investment income.)

- The seller is likely to achieve a targeted IRR that compensates them for the risk of holding subordinated notes.

C Corporation Alternative 2: Day Loan Strategy

A second structure is available to sellers in ESOP transactions who want to take advantage of Section 1042. As indicated above, the scope of this chapter does not address the requirements of Section 1042 but rather the investment unit strategies that can be used in connection with Section 1042 transactions.

The ESOP sponsor will borrow 100% of the transaction purchase price from a third-party senior lender on a short-term basis. The loan proceeds are then loaned to the ESOP, which uses the funds to purchase 100% of the company's issued and outstanding stock from the selling shareholders. The selling shareholders then deposit the sale proceeds in blocked bank accounts offered by the third-party lender. The funds stay in the blocked account for a short period of time, usually one day to one week. Following the expiration of the deposit period, the funds are used to purchase an investment unit from the issuer for cash.

Taxpayers using the day loan structure must thoroughly understand the application and implications of the investment unit rule and the rules governing original issue discount (OID) found in Code Sections 1272, 1273, and 1274. Failure to appropriately design the day loan structure can result in disadvantageous income tax consequences to the selling shareholders. The advantages of the day loan include:

- Compliance with the provisions of Section 1042 will result in the deferral of the gain realized in the transaction.

- The ACA tax on income will not apply because Section 1411(C) defines net investment income as net gain (to the extent taken into account in computing taxable income) attributable to the disposition of property. If a Section 1042 election is made with respect to the shares sold, no gain will be recognized. If no gain is recognized, the realized gain will not be taken into account in computing taxable income.

- The proceeds, if any, received from the warrants will be taxed as long-term capital gain.

- This strategy requires careful planning to avoid OID.

S Corporation Structure: ESOP Purchase Coupled with a Redemption

A typical S corporation ESOP transaction may involve an ESOP purchasing for cash a percentage of the shares offered in the transaction. The number of shares purchased in the transaction is driven by the issuer's cash and access to senior debt. Often the ESOP purchase is 30% of the value of the offered shares. The exact amount of the ESOP purchase portion of the transaction normally equals the issuer's senior debt capacity. The remaining offered shares are redeemed in exchange for an investment unit. This strategy results in the ESOP owning 100% of the issued and outstanding stock of the issuer. The advantages of this structure include:

- The transaction gain will be reported as long-term capital gain using the installment method, assuming the seller meets the holding period requirement and other capital gain requirements.
- The seller may be able to avoid the imposition of the 3.8% Medicare surtax on investment income imposed by Code Section 1411. A careful analysis must be made as to whether sellers are engaged in a trade or business to which the tax applies (see 1411(c)(4)). Assuming the seller is an active participant in a pass-through entity (e.g., an S corporation), the tax will not apply.
- The warrants will provide the selling shareholders with a market yield commensurate with the risk of holding subordinate notes.
- Assuming the company meets its forecast, the sellers will achieve the targeted IRR.
- The warrant proceeds will be taxed at long-term capital gain rates.
- This strategy normally does not implicate OID because the investment unit is issued for non-publicly traded property.

Benefits of Warrant Structure in ESOP Transactions to the Fiduciary and Issuer

Warrants are neither intrinsically a good or bad idea from a fiduciary or issuer standpoint. Some of the pros include:

- In ESOP transactions, warrants are used to increase yield when, for whatever reason, an increased coupon is not possible or desirable.
- Selling shareholders are prepared to accept warrants in lieu of a higher interest rate on the note for the following reasons:
  — The issuer does not have the cash flow to support paying a higher interest rate in cash.
  — The seller is willing to accept the risk and rewards of an equity-like investment.
  — Sellers are taxed at long-term capital gain rates on warrant yield as opposed to ordinary income rates on interest.

Fiduciaries often prefer warrant coverage instead of higher stated interest rates on a seller notes because cash flow necessary to fund the stated interest is reduced. The ESOP is protected in the event the company is not successful. The warrants will provide additional yield to the sellers only if the company meets or exceeds its projections. If the company hits a home run, everyone is happy. The warrant structure provides the company and the ESOP with access to financing that otherwise would not be available or would be prohibitively expensive.

The overall yield on the investment units often exceeds the yield the seller could receive by investing in conventional securities.

On the other hand, warrants can be structured too aggressively, and the DOL often focuses on deals with warrants that it believes yield too high a return. Pushing the envelope on assumptions can make these deals more likely to be investigated and/or litigated. Warrants in a successful company can also create a one-time very high redemption cost that the company must be prepared to pay on top of what may be a growing repurchase obligation.

I would like to thank the following people for their assistance and contribution with the preparation of this chapter: James Moser of Foster Garvey PC, Kim Blaugher of the Beyster Institute, and Lynn DuBois of the ESOP Law Group.

Chapter 7

Alternative Financing Sources in ESOP Transactions

Dan Kaczmarek

The purpose of this chapter is to describe alternative financing sources for transactions involving ESOP-owned companies. Transactions can be related to initial ESOP transactions, partial-to-full ESOP transactions, growth initiatives/acquisitions, or a myriad of other purposes. The type of alternative capital chosen depends on many things, including the amount of capital needed, the company's cash flow or collateral coverage, strategic objectives, and uses of the capital. This chapter also explores what key stakeholders should consider before seeking these alternatives. This chapter does not discuss traditional financing sources in ESOP transactions. Throughout the chapter, "traditional financing sources" refers to senior bank debt and seller notes with detachable warrants.

Why Is There a Need for Alternative Financing?

When pursuing an ESOP transaction (or any type of balance sheet recapitalization), alternative financing sources may need to be explored beyond traditional financing sources. This could be for a variety of reasons. First, a larger amount of capital or liquidity may be sought, which could trigger the need to speak with alternative capital providers. Traditional capital providers may be willing to provide only a certain amount of capital for their perceived risk-taking. Second, traditional sources of capital may not be available or willing to provide capital. A particular company's characteristics or dynamics may limit the willingness of traditional financing sources to provide capital. For example, a business may operate in an out-of-favor industry, or the perceived riskiness of a business may be beyond a certain comfort level for providers. Further, macroeconomic conditions in the broader market environment may cause providers to be more cautious and unwilling to provide capital. This has clearly been seen during the Great Recession in the late 2000s and more recently with the COVID-19 pandemic. Finally, the company may be seeking a more customized capital structure to meet specific goals or objectives in a transaction. For example, scenarios exist whereby a company is seeking a more mechanical or structured program for future capital borrowings. Traditional capital sources may not be willing to agree to this structure in advance. Alternative financing sources, on the other hand, can be more creative and customize credit or equity facilities to meet these objectives.

There are many reasons why alternative financing sources may be ideal for a company to pursue. The reasons and examples listed above are just a few that exist. The key takeaway is that if a traditional financing source is unwilling or unable to provide capital, one should not get discouraged since there are a myriad of alternative financing providers who stand ready to help companies achieve their goals and objectives.

What Alternative Financing Options Exist?

Many alternative financing options exist. This section is not meant to be all-encompassing and is focused on some of the typical, more common forms of alternative financing options available.

Mezzanine Debt

Mezzanine debt is the middle layer of capital that sits subordinated to senior debt and above equity on the balance sheet. This type of capital is usually not secured by assets and is lent based on a company's ability to repay with cash flows. This form of capital is a great way to bridge the gap between the company's cash needs and what traditional lenders are willing to provide. This is often described as more "patient" capital. Mezzanine debt does not require any principal payments and simply has a balloon payment at the end of its term. This debt typically matures six months or more after any senior debt on the balance sheet. Because this debt sits lower on the balance sheet, it is deemed to be riskier than senior debt and requires higher interest rates. As such, it is common for interest rates for this type of debt to be double digits and to have a component of it be "payment in kind" (PIK). This means that the interest is not paid in cash but added to the principal balance of the mezzanine debt instrument. Some benefits of mezzanine debt include: no amortization, longer maturity, and providing additional liquidity and or capital without diluting existing owners. Some considerations include higher interest costs, prepayment penalties if one desires to repay the debt sooner than required, stricter financial covenants, and, in some cases, board of directors observation rights and/or seats. Sources for mezzanine capital include traditional commercial banks, nonbank lending institutions, insurance companies, and some private equity firms.

Structured or Preferred Equity

Structured equity or preferred equity represents flexible capital that has debt- and equity-like characteristics. This capital sits below debt and above common equity on the balance sheet. It is often labeled as "structured" equity because it is not common equity and usually has incremental features compared to common equity. For example, this type of capital may have a principal component and accruing dividend component (like debt). It may even have a required return component. Further, this capital may have an equity participation component, such as conversion into common equity. In these instances, the accrued dividends may be eliminated, and only common equity is held, or the common equity may be incremental to the dividends. The capital is placed on the balance sheet with call and put features. A call right is the company's ability to buy back the equity. A put right is the equity holder's ability to force the company to buy back the equity. The time periods for the call and put features, as well as determining the fair market value of the equity, are subject to negotiations with the capital provider. This capital provides incremental liquidity or capital beyond bank and mezzanine debt. However, structured equity is dilutive to the existing equity holders of the business. This form of capital will also typically require observation rights or actual seats on the company's board of directors. The other terms and conditions of structured equity are subject to market conditions and negotiations. Common negotiated terms include reporting requirements, anti-dilutive provisions, and conversion features, among others. Sources of structured equity include nonbank lending institutions, insurance companies, and private equity.

Common Equity

Common equity or common stock represents the most basic form of ownership in a company. Investors in this scenario are holding the same class of stock as the ESOP. All characteristics of their investment mirror the stock held by the ESOP. Common equity investors participate in the performance of the company, the value of which will move up and down. Common equity investors benefit from dividends and equity value growth. Common stock is subordinate to all other capital (debt through preferred equity). Common stock is the riskiest form of investment and provides the holder with unlimited upside. Common stock is dilutive to the existing owners of the company and typically comes with a requirement for seats on the company's board of directors. Common equity investors will be entitled to receive information and vote the company's shares as directed in its bylaws. Some common equity investors can be vocal and attempt to sway strategic directions of the company; other investors will be more passive in nature. Sources of common equity are typically private equity firms.

What Are Structuring Considerations When Choosing Alternative Financing Options?

Understanding that there are alternative financing sources is helpful. However, choosing which alternative financing source is most appropriate gets more complicated. The key stakeholders in a company or transaction must explore the various considerations to identify the best form of capital. This discussion focuses on three key stakeholders: the company, the owner/seller, and the ESOP trustee. The intent of this section is to provide thought-provoking questions and color as one considers alternative forms of capital.

Company Considerations

There are several things to think about in choosing a debt structure:

- Will the contemplated capital structure enable the company to execute its strategy? Stated differently, does this capital help the company achieve its strategic goals and objectives as an organization? For example, if the company's goal is to acquire smaller competitors, the capital placed in the transaction should be supportive of acquiring future targets. A common equity investor, for instance, may have more appetite to fund these acquisitions in the future than a traditional commercial bank.

- Will cash flow be available to reinvest in the business? Can the company support debt servicing? It is important to choose a capital structure that is not so onerous that the company cannot meet its debt servicing obligations. Not only must a company be able to meet its debt obligations, but there should be enough cash flow to execute on corporate strategies as well. If a company can barely meet any debt servicing obligations from a selected capital structure, the company may want to reconsider the contemplated structure.

- Will leadership be forced to sell the company in the future in order to pay back the capital provider? There may be a balloon payment for mezzanine debt or a required repayment of an equity investor in the future. The company must be able to afford these obligations through cash generated or through a refinancing with other debt providers. A company should know going into an alternative financing transaction exactly how it plans to repay the debt or equity obligations when due. Selling the company may be the only option in the future, and this may conflict with the company's strategic plan.

- What financial covenants and reporting are required? As previously mentioned, certain types of debt and/or equity provide benefits, but also come with financial covenants and reporting requirements. Is the company prepared to provide monthly reporting to a mezzanine debt provider? Is a company prepared to offer a board seat to an equity investor?

- Does decision-making and control change? By taking on alternative capital, there could be changes to the decision-makers in an organization. In some instances, the individuals may be the same, but servicing debt obligations may now be a top priority. In situations where there is a legal change in control, is the strategic direction the same of the new owners compared to the previous?

- If the company wants to be 100% ESOP-owned, any equity investment structured as common stock will mean the company loses that status and will have to make distribution to the equity holder(s). It may be possible to provide the equity holder with some form of synthetic equity or with warrants. In addition, other structuring options exist using multiple legal entities and classes of stock.

Owner/Seller Considerations

Sellers have a number of considerations specific to them, including:

- Will the capital structure provide sufficient cash at close? Many owners have a liquidity goal when transacting. In some instances, there needs to be sufficient liquidity at close to owners to justify selling or recapitalizing a business. A traditional provider of capital may not provide the desired levels. As previously discussed, several forms of alternative capital can increase liquidity at close and effectively meet this objective.

- How involved will the seller be post-transaction? Sellers may be looking for maximum liquidity and be willing to "take a back seat" of running the business. If this is the case, they may be willing to give up legal control. If the seller will be very involved post-closing, they may not want the reporting or financial covenants associated with certain types of alternative capital providers. They may fear that these requirements will divert management's attention from operational objectives.

- Do investment returns and creditor or equity rights match risk? Owners will be "giving up" something for the increased capital and liquidity. In some instances, it is increased borrowing costs in the form of interest expense on mezzanine debt. In other instances, it is an ownership interest in the operations to a preferred or common equity provider. A seller or business owner needs to ask whether "what I am receiving outweighs what I am giving up."

- Does decision-making and control change? Will there be a new board member or observer voicing concerns or guidance for the operations? If so, does the owner have a preexisting relationship with this person or firm? Will there be friction at the board level? Conversely, what positive attributes can this individual bring? A new board member may have experience in the industry or have previously been a part of transactions of this type.

Trustee Considerations

Finally, trustees have to be comfortable with the overall fairness to plan participants of the deal structure, as well as any imprudent risks the structure may entail. They should ask:

- Does the capital structure create an insolvency risk? A trustee is a fiduciary of plan assets, which hold the equity of a company. If the capital structure will put the equity at risk, a trustee may not be okay with the transaction.
- Is the debt or equity priced at market rates and terms? A trustee will want to ensure that any capital used in the transaction is not dilutive to the ESOP. If it is dilutive, is the ESOP receiving a benefit in the transaction?
- Does decision-making and control change? If an equity capital provider is coming into the capital structure and taking control, the ESOP must receive adequate consideration.
- How is employees' long-term value affected? ESOP trustees will view capital structure decisions as a fiduciary. If employees' value will be harmed from a capital markets transaction, an ESOP trustee will need to understand the rationale.

Each stakeholder will have its own set of considerations to weigh before transacting with alternative sources of capital. In some instances, interests will be aligned, and, in some instances, interests may conflict. For a successful outcome, full transparency of considerations is encouraged among all parties.

Tips for Successful Alternative Financing Transactions

As previously mentioned, there are several alternative capital providers, and the form and structure of capital can vary. Though no transaction is identical, a company and management team can take certain measures to ensure a successful outcome regardless of the capital and structure selected.

First, as discussed above, all stakeholders should fully understand the goals and objectives and consider whether the transaction would achieve or hurt those objectives. These objectives should be identified before starting any transaction and communicated to all parties involved. For example, a capital provider who understands the uses of capital may better structure a solution to meet the intended objectives. Second, a company should hire experienced advisors to lead the transaction. Advisors should have knowledge of the various capital providers and structuring solutions. In addition, advisors should have relevant experience in the same industry in which the company operates and have executed upon similar types of transactions. Finally, a company needs to be fully prepared for what a transaction process entails. Preparation items can include, but are not limited to (1) preparing a five-year business plan forecast, (2) reviewing the company's state of accounting records and financial control systems, and (3) preparing to market the company as one would its own products and services to prospective customers. Further, these types of transactions take time, and a company should plan for and allow adequate time to explore the financing alternatives.

Alternative financing providers are not new to the ESOP marketplace. Companies should consider this source of capital if it helps achieve the goals and objectives. However, like any corporate or strategic decision, proper education, exploration, and preparation is necessary to ensure a successful outcome.

About the Authors

Regina Carls is the managing director of the ESOP advisory group at J.P. Morgan. She is dedicated to helping bankers and their privately held clients evaluate the benefits of selling stock to an ESOP and therefore creating liquidity for the owners in the transaction. Regina was responsible for the initial development of the ESOP advisory group. She quickly became a liaison with all areas of the firm, assisting in the analysis and structuring of complex ESOP financings.

Philip (P.J.) Carstens is an attorney with Foster Garvey PC and has more than 40 years of experience advising clients on a wide array of complex business matters, including mergers, reorganizations, acquisitions, and other financial transactions. He is recognized as one of the nation's most experienced attorneys in the design and implementation of ESOPs and other plans governed by ERISA. P.J. is recognized by The Best Lawyers in America and is a member of the NCEO and the ESOP Association, as well as a frequent presenter on ESOP-related topics. He earned his LL.M. in taxation from New York University School of Law and his J.D. from University of San Francisco School of Law.

Vaughn Gordy is the non-executive chairman of the board and retired chief executive officer of GreatBanc Trust Company and has 25 years' experience in the ESOP trustee business. Mr. Gordy is also an author and speaker on many ESOP issues as well as a member of the ESOP Association, the National Center for Employee Ownership (NCEO), National Association of Corporate Directors (NACD) and Employee-Owned S Corporations of America (ESCA).

Dan Kaczmarek is an investment banker within the corporate finance group at Chartwell Financial Advisory. He is responsible for business development and execution of debt/equity capital-raising transactions and sales of privately held businesses to strategic acquirers, private equity firms, and ESOPs. Dan has worked on a myriad of successful M&A, capital markets, and ESOP transactions within the industries of consumer products, food products, business services, healthcare, manufacturing, transportation/logistics, and technology, among others. Dan is a member and frequent speaker for the ESOP Association, National Center for Employee Ownership, and the American Council of Engineering Companies. He is a registered representative with Chartwell affiliate CCS Transactions, LLC, and holds FINRA Series 63 and 79 licenses. Dan earned a BS in business administration with concentrations in finance and legal studies from the University of Miami in Coral Gables, Florida.

Bill Merten is a partner at Winston & Strawn LLP, chairs its ESOP practice, and focuses his practice on business succession planning and executive compensation. He advises corporations, shareholders, directors, and various professionals regarding the use of stock-based compensation, ESOPs, and ESOP-related strategies in a wide variety of transactions, including management buyouts, ownership succession transactions, private equity transactions, going-private transactions, ESOP company sales, and mergers and acquisitions. Bill is a fellow of the American College of Employee Benefits Counsel (ACEBC) and has been recognized by a variety of publications, such as Martindale-Hubbell, *American Lawyer Media, Super Lawyers, The Legal 500,* and Leading Lawyers Network.

Scott Rodrick is the director of publishing and information technology at the National Center for Employee Ownership (NCEO). He designed and created the NCEO's present line of publications and is the author or coauthor of several books himself, including the bestselling *An Introduction to ESOPs* (19th ed. 2020). He created the NCEO's first website in 1994 and since then has been involved with the NCEO's presence on the Internet. He is an attorney and served at the U.S. Department of Labor as an attorney-advisor before coming to the NCEO.

Corey Rosen founded the NCEO in 1981 after working for five years as a professional staff member in the U.S. Senate, where he helped draft legislation on employee ownership plans. Before that, he taught political science at Ripon College. He is the author or coauthor of many books and over 100 articles on employee ownership, and coauthor (with John Case and Martin Staubus) of *Equity: Why Employee Ownership Is Good for Business* (Harvard Business School Press, 2005). He was the subject of an extensive interview in *Inc.* magazine in August 2000; has appeared frequently on CNN, PBS, NPR, and other network programs; and is regularly quoted in the *Wall Street Journal,* the *New York Times,* and other leading publications. He has a Ph.D. in political science from Cornell University. He serves on a number of ESOP company boards and continues active involvement with the NCEO as a member of the staff.

David B. Solomon is a partner and chairman of the corporate practice of Levenfeld Pearlstein, LLC, headquartered in Chicago, Illinois. David also founded and serves as the head of the firm's ESOP practice, which serves clients who are involved in various types of transactions involving ESOPs. David is a member of the NCEO's board of directors and has lectured frequently and published articles in several publications on various ESOP-related topics.

About the NCEO

The National Center for Employee Ownership (NCEO) is a nonprofit organization that has supported the employee ownership community since 1981. Our mission is to help employee ownership thrive. We have more than 3,000 members because we help people make smart decisions about employee ownership, with everything from reliable information on technical issues to helping companies reach the full potential of employee ownership.

We generate original research, facilitate the exchange of best practices at our live and online events, feature the best and most current writing by experts in our publications, and help employee ownership companies build ownership cultures where employees think and act like owners.

Membership Benefits

NCEO members receive the following benefits and more:

- The members-only newsletter *Employee Ownership Report.*
- Access to the NCEO's members-only website resources, including the Document Library, ESOP Q&A, and more.
- Free access to both live and recorded webinars.
- Discounts on books and other NCEO products and services.
- The right to contact the NCEO for answers to questions.

To join as a member, order publications, or find more resources and data on ESOPs and employee ownership, visit www.nceo.org or call us at 510-208-1300.

Made in United States
North Haven, CT
18 July 2023